Terror in the Adirondacks

Terror in the Adirondacks

The True Story of Serial Killer Robert F. Garrow

Lawrence P. Gooley

Bloated Toe Publishing
Peru, New York 12972

Other books by the author:

A History of the Altona Flat Rock
Lyon Mountain: The Tragedy of a Mining Town
Out of the Darkness: In Memory of Lyon Mountain's Iron Men
The Battle of Plattsburgh Question & Answer Book
A History of the Altona Flat Rock – Silver Anniversary Edition
Brendler's Boys: The House That George Built
Oliver's War: An Adirondack Rebel Battles the Rockefeller Fortune
History of Churubusco and the Town of Clinton, Clinton County, New York
Adirondack & North Country Gold: 50+ New & True Stories You're Sure to Love
25 Diabolical Adirondack Murders: The Twisted, Fiendish Deeds of North Country Killers
Killing in the Kuyahoora Valley—A True Story: The Murder of Poland, New York,
Schoolteacher Lydia Beecher by Teenager Jean Gianini
Escape from Dannemora: 170 Years of Escapes, Tortures, and Infamous Inmates at
New York's Most Notorious Prison

People & Places of the Adirondacks & Foothills—VOLUME 1

People & Places of the Adirondacks & Foothills—VOLUME 2

People & Places of the Adirondacks & Foothills—VOLUME 3

People & Places of the Adirondacks & Foothills—VOLUME 4

People & Places of the Adirondacks & Foothills—VOLUME 5

People & Places of the Adirondacks & Foothills—VOLUME 6

People & Places of the Adirondacks & Foothills—VOLUME 7

Bloated Toe Publishing, Peru, NY 12972

Library of Congress Control Number: 2009930558
ISBN-13: 978-0-9795741-3-9   ISBN-10: 0-9795741-3-7

Copies of this title and the titles listed above may be obtained by writing to:
Bloated Toe Enterprises, PO Box 324, Peru, NY 12972
or
Go to Bloated Toe Enterprises website:
www.bloatedtoe.com   info@bloatedtoe.com

Both covers were created by Jill C. Jones and Lawrence P. Gooley

Printed and bound by Versa Press, Inc., East Peoria, IL
Manufactured in the United States of America

Contents

Preface

The Robert F. Garrow story is a hellish, frightful, sad part of Adirondack history. But it *is* part of history. Witherbee residents have expressed anger and dismay in the past when the story resurfaced periodically in the media. In like fashion, some of them may be upset by the appearance of this book.

However, it is not a retelling of their own personal story, and it did not solely affect them. It altered the balance of life in the Adirondacks, killing permanently for many of us the innocence of a summer outing. I am among that group.

I was twenty years old and an enthusiastic mountain climber when Garrow struck in 1973. Immediately attitudes changed, and the general presumption of safety vanished. With a sense of defiance, I continued to climb, but the effects of Garrow's crimes were life-changing.

Every single time another hiker was encountered, there was a slight feeling of fear and trepidation as we approached each other. We mumbled nervous "hellos" as we passed. Many of us carried some sort of weapon in our pocket or backpack. I knew then that the mountains would never feel the same for me.

I refused to let Garrow steal completely from me a very special part of life. Since then, I've enjoyed several hundred additional climbs. I've hiked, biked, and canoed, with more than a thousand miles in each category. The thrills and pleasures were immeasurable, and I always felt lucky to have such a fantastic playground at my doorstep.

But never have I felt completely safe. There was always that nagging memory of what could, and did, happen, all thanks to Robert Garrow.

Despite my revulsion for Garrow's abhorrent acts, innate curiosity drew me to his story, which has stayed with me for more than three decades. Today details of his life and crimes can be viewed on websites and are occasionally repeated in newspapers. The adjoining issue of Garrow's lawyers and their national ethics battle is likewise covered.

I can offer assurance that nowhere has the tale been told with accuracy, even in abbreviated accounts. Assumptions were made, and facts have been distorted through repetition over the years. Some participants in the saga have offered accounts decades later that differ from the original rendition, and from the official court chronicle.

Parts of the story have sometimes been changed in an apparent effort at dramatization. After perusing the record, I can't imagine why anyone would attempt to enhance a true story containing more twists than the wildest of Hollywood concoctions.

Terror in the Adirondacks is based on official records, including 2,000 pages of court transcripts; birth, marriage, and death records; census records; and various files from related court cases. That information has been supported by more than eight hundred newspaper and magazine articles, plus journals, prison records, personal interviews, and the final official report on Robert Garrow issued by the NYS Department of Correctional Services.

I would like to express acknowledgment and thanks to Hamilton County Clerk Jane Zarecki and her staff for their kind treatment; the Syracuse Newspapers Photo Archive; and the NYS Education Department.

Special thanks to my partner, Jill Jones, for assistance every step of the way.

1

Blood in the Mountains

On Friday, July 20, 1973, the body of a young man was found just off Route 8 in rural Warren County, New York, near Wevertown in the southern Adirondack Mountains. Police said the victim had been stabbed to death, a shocking revelation.

That sort of thing just didn't happen in the Adirondack Park, a spectacular natural playground in northern New York State. The park itself is massive, consisting of six million acres, equal to the combined total size of Everglades, Grand Canyon, Smoky Mountain, and Yellowstone National Parks.

The Olympic Village of Lake Placid is a major tourist attraction in the Adirondacks, and the easy accessibility of the wilderness draws many visitors to the region. Thousands of people vacation in the mountains every year to get away from it all, to get back in touch with nature, and to share the fun, relaxed atmosphere with family and friends.

Murder in the Adirondacks is a rarity, and as news of the crime first surfaced, people were naturally alarmed. In the relative safety of the mountains, perhaps domestic violence could explain such a deviation from the tranquil norm. In this case, police suspected otherwise, and as details began to surface, people became much more fearful.

The victim had sustained four stab wounds, including two to the heart. But there was more to this crime than murder. Police quickly confirmed the identity of the young man as Daniel Porter, 22, of Concord, Massachusetts. They also learned that he had not been traveling alone.

Porter's girlfriend, Susan Petz of Skokie, Illinois, had accompanied him on the trip into the Adirondacks, where they planned to do some whitewater rafting on the upper Hudson

River. The two were last seen together on Saturday, July 14 in Amsterdam, just south of the Adirondacks, and had not returned from their adventure as scheduled.

Just two months prior to the mountain excursion, Daniel Porter had graduated from Harvard University. Like many others who watched America struggle through the war in Vietnam, Porter had been on track to change the world. Young people strongly supported Senator George McGovern's bid for the presidency in 1972, and his message resonated with Porter and his peers.

McGovern's outspoken anti-war stance was attractive to the college crowd, prompting many to become involved in the political process. Daniel Porter, with fellow Harvard seniors Pat Caddell and John Gorman, founded Cambridge Survey Research, Inc., the company that did the polling for McGovern's campaign, and would handle Jimmy Carter's in his 1976 election bid.

The growing firm was destined to one day merge with other large, similar companies, eventually owning offices in more than fifty countries. It all should have been part of Daniel Porter's future.

Now, Porter was dead and Susan Petz was missing. Authorities soon learned that, several days earlier, passing motorists had seen Porter's car parked off the roadway. The victim was deceased by that time, so when police finally made the grisly discovery, the crime scene was already several days old. The coroner was busy trying to determine the exact date of Porter's death.

Immediately a search was launched, focusing on the surrounding woods. It was difficult to be hopeful, considering the situation. The doors of Porter's white BMW were found locked, and some of Petz's personal items remained in the vehicle, indicating she had left the site quickly and unwillingly. There seemed an excellent chance that troopers would find Petz in the woods nearby, possibly the victim of rape and murder.

The first hours of searching turned up nothing of value, prompting police to summon more resources. A helicopter was brought in, but the dense foliage of July's Adirondacks rendered aerial views ineffective. Bloodhounds were put to the test, probing futilely for any scent trail. Hours turned into days, and the outlook was grim.

Hope for a successful conclusion dwindled further when a local citizen claimed he had murdered Petz and dumped her body in a beaver flow (an area flooded by a beaver dam). Police viewed the supposed confession with suspicion, but out of necessity, searchers spent many difficult hours wading in swamps and marshy conditions. Their efforts yielded nothing, and the claim proved bogus.

As the search entered its fifth day, the use of hounds was abandoned. The coroner's findings revealed that Porter had actually been murdered at least three days before his body was found. By now, a full week had passed since the crime had been committed, including several days of heavy rain. Even if the perpetrator had left a trail, the bloodhounds had precious little to work with.

A team of forest rangers, conservation officers, sheriff's deputies, and state police, bolstered by volunteers, continued the ground search. But even with fifty men scouring the area for days, nothing was found.

The body of Susan Petz might still lie somewhere in the surrounding dense woods, but officials believed it was far more likely she had been abducted. Some evidence at the scene supported that theory, and the fruitless ground search gave further credence to the kidnapping scenario.

Police efforts to solve the crime explored a number of possibilities even as the hunt for Petz continued. But more than a week after Porter's body was found, there was still no explanation for the tragic events that had occurred along this lonesome Adirondack road. With the passage of time and no additional evidence, the story seemed doomed to fade from the headlines, destined for the cold case file.

But that didn't happen. On Sunday morning, July 29, just nine days after Porter's body was discovered, word came of another attack.

Four young friends were on a summer camping trip in the mountains, and had pitched their tents along a remote section of Old Route 8 between the villages of Speculator and Wells.

The group consisted of Philip Domblewski, 18, who had just graduated from Mont Pleasant High School in Schenectady; Nicholas Fiorillo, 20, and David Freeman, 19, both also from Schenectady; and Freeman's girlfriend, Carol Ann Malinowski, 23, of Amsterdam, New York.

Their original plan was to stay at a campground in Wells, but by the time they arrived on Saturday night, there were no vacancies. Under a heavy Adirondack rain, the group headed north of Wells at about 10:30 p.m. Finding a suitable roadside location a few miles north of the village, they set up their tents with the aid of the cars' lights and settled in for the night.

Domblewski and Fiorillo, who shared one of the tents, awoke at about 6:00 a.m. on Sunday to get an early start on a planned fishing excursion. Once dressed, they took down their tent and loaded it into Fiorillo's car. Before departing, they asked Freeman and Malinowksi to join them, but the couple preferred to sleep in, so the two young men drove off in search of a warm breakfast before doing some fishing.

Heading south through Wells and on to Northville, they satisfied their hunger at a local restaurant. The two then traveled north on Route 30, purchased bait in the hamlet of Hope, and arrived back at the campsite around 8:00 a.m.

Once again, the pair spoke to David Freeman through the walls of the tent, but he declined to join them just yet. They left a container of worms on the ground for him and again took to the road. About a half mile away, the two young men left the parked car and spent the better part of the next hour fishing.

Back at the campsite, Freeman and Malinowski were still in their tent, not yet dressed after a night's sleep. Carol was wearing only panties, and David wore underpants and an undershirt. The screening on the tent was zipped shut, and the main tent flap was closed but untied.

Malinowski soon heard footsteps approaching, and without warning, the tent flap opened wide. A stranger, holding a rifle and wearing binoculars around his neck, squatted at the opening, positioning himself about halfway inside the tent. Both Carol and David were startled by the man's sudden appearance. Carol made an effort to cover herself, and Freeman asked what he wanted.

The man said his car had run out of gas, and he wanted to siphon some fuel from their vehicle. He told them to hurry and get dressed before their friends came back, adding somewhat ominously that nobody would get hurt if they cooperated.

Freeman was dressed within five minutes, but Carol had problems, unable to find her glasses or her sandals. With David's help, and the man pressing them to rush, they finally found everything and began to leave the tent.

Just then a car pulled up, visible to both the stranger and Carol, who was exiting the tent in front of David. The man gestured with the rifle, indicating they should step back inside, and then motioned for the two men in the car to come and join him. It was Fiorillo and Domblewski, returning from their fishing trip.

As Fiorillo parked the car, he and Domblewski saw the man near the tent and wondered what was going on. When he waved them over, they left the car and walked down to the clearing.

As they neared the tent, the man stood up, and for the first time they realized he was carrying a rifle and wearing binoculars. The immediate assumption was that he was some type of forest ranger. That idea was quickly dispelled.

The couple was ordered to come out of the tent, and a brief conversation ensued. The four campers were told the man was being pursued by police and the FBI, and needed gas for his car. Carol's vehicle was parked nearby, along with Nick's. Considering the situation, there was little they could do to stop him. At that point, the robbery seemed a foregone conclusion.

But there was more. The man kept talking, and his words instilled terror. They were now witnesses to his presence in the area and couldn't be trusted to maintain silence. To ensure secrecy, he would have to tie them up in the woods.

Using the lever action of the weapon to eject a live shell, he made it clear that the gun was loaded and he meant business. With the rifle as intimidation, he guided them away from the tent site.

Now on the highway, they were told to walk along the road. All the while, their minds raced collectively, seeking a way out.

Maybe the stranger did plan to tie them up, steal some gas, and make his escape. But, instinctively wary of that assessment, the four of them began to talk, hoping to reason with him.

Fiorillo proffered a set of keys, offering his car to the stranger, whose only response was "Be quiet and keep walking." Despite that admonition, they kept trying, fearful of what might befall them. He ignored their pleas, and finally injected a sinister note: "I've killed before and I'll kill again." With that, anxiety gave way to fear and dread.

Crossing the highway, they were shepherded to a narrow woods road leading to a clearing. After following another path for a short distance, perhaps twenty feet, their captor said, "This place isn't right; it's not good enough."

Directed back to the clearing, they were steered farther along to a second road. At gunpoint, they again entered the woods and were soon enveloped in the thick forest, well beyond the view of any passing motorists.

In such heavy cover, it might prove difficult to keep track of the group. To preempt any thoughts of escape, a warning was issued. If they tried anything, he would "blow a hole in them."

For a few minutes, they walked deeper into the woods. The man apologized to Carol for her wet, muddied sandals, and lamented the thick brush and the bothersome bugs. Though he seemed to be making conversation at times, other comments were intended to spark fear, including frequent reminders that he had already killed.

Despite repeated threats, the stranger's demeanor remained relatively calm. Encouraged by this, they again offered their cars to him. When that didn't work, Fiorillo took a different approach, searching for some common ground. They had been in trouble with the law, he claimed, and could sympathize with the man's situation.

But no matter what they tried, all of their efforts failed. Finally, when the dense cover thinned briefly, the group was ordered to stop. Here was a suitable place to tie them up.

An ominous sequence of events began to unfold. Their abductor gestured toward a tree, indicating someone should be seated. Phil Domblewski stepped forward and sat down with his back against the trunk. The man unsheathed his knife, cut a piece of rope, and handed it to Freeman, instructing him to tie Domblewski to the tree.

Nick and Phil renewed their pleas with an increased sense of urgency, but it was no use. Domblewski was told to sit facing away from the woods road, and to put his hands around the tree behind him. The man observed as Freeman tied the rope to one of Domblewski's wrists with two knots, and then, with some slack between the hands, fastened it similarly to the other wrist. Freeman was sternly warned, "That had better be tight, because I'm coming back to check the ropes."

The rest of the group moved another fifty feet towards the woods road, out of sight of Domblewski. There, the process was repeated, this time with Freeman tying Fiorillo to a tree. Nick was positioned facing the road, away from Phil. Both young men were tied in the same manner, with their backs against the tree trunks. Again came the warning to Freeman that the ropes had better be tight.

The three of them probed deeper into the woods, where Carol tied Freeman to a tree. David was forced to sit in the same position as his two friends, but could see neither of them. Fiorillo was fifty feet away, while Domblewski was about eighty feet distant.

Carol struggled nervously, trying to tie the knots, and the stranger became upset with the delay. He ordered Freeman to give her instructions, and after a short lesson, she completed the job, receiving the same stern warning that the ropes had better be tight.

Malinowski was now the only one left. He marched her back in the direction of where Fiorillo and Domblewski were restrained. It was time to select a tree for Carol.

Despite repeated threats to check the tightness of the ropes, they walked past Fiorillo without stopping. Carol was ordered to pick out her own tree, and as she looked around through the woods, Nick could be seen to her left and Phil to her right. Her first choice was too close to Domblewski's tree, and the stranger rejected it. Moving a little farther away, she made a second choice that was deemed acceptable.

As her companions had done, Carol sat by the tree, terrified of what was to come. The stranger proceeded to tie her wrists together, all the while engaging her in conversation. He noted the absence of a wedding ring from her finger, and upon learning she wasn't married, asked, "What would your parents think?" Then, he told her, "I'm going to come back and take you with me, and I'll probably let you go."

The man retrieved his knife and rifle, both of which he had left on the ground while securing Malinowski to the tree. Silently, he walked off towards Domblewski.

From where Carol was seated, she had a partial view of Phil, and could now see the man positioned in front of him. They were talking in what seemed to be normal tones, but the words remained indistinguishable.

Then, alarmingly, Malinowski heard a gagging, vomiting sound coming from the same direction. She could see Phil, apparently still seated, with his hands tied behind the tree, and the stranger bending over him.

Nervously, she called out to Domblewski to see if he was all right. With no immediate reply, she called out again, demanding an answer. The response came from the stranger, who yelled at her to be quiet, followed by "You'll be all right, when it's all over with, you'll be all right, just a little bit longer, you'll be all right."

Panic gripped Carol as she heard inhuman sounds coming from Domblewski's direction. The steady vomiting sound morphed into occasional choking, gurgling noises, which lasted for a couple of minutes.

Carol was seated alone against a tree, but she wasn't alone in what she was hearing. Nick Fiorillo was also within earshot. He noticed his friend's voice starting to rise in pitch, and Phil seemed to be talking rapidly.

Nick heard the same vomiting, retching sounds, followed by a verbal exchange between Malinowski and their captor. Though he couldn't hear everything that was said, Fiorillo felt certain that the man had done something terrible to Phil.

The panic that gripped Carol also struck Nick, and he worked hard at getting free of his restraints. Struggling feverishly, the anxiety built as he loosened his bonds, all the while listening to

Domblewski's choking, gasping sounds.

Again he heard the stranger talk, followed by silence, and then a vomiting sound lasting twenty seconds or more. In near hysteria now, Fiorillo freed himself and broke into a wild sprint in the direction of the highway, hoping to reach his car.

Malinowski still observed the stranger near Domblewski's tree, her view partially obstructed by foliage. Sudden noises in the forest distracted her attention for a moment. She thought, and hoped, that one of the men had managed to escape. The sounds were, in fact, those of Fiorillo racing for freedom. The stranger seemed not to notice, so intense was his focus on Phil.

Domblewski, tied up and totally defenseless, continued to emit frightening sounds that Carol could hear. After another minute, the sounds became intermittent, and finally, they stopped altogether.

During Fiorillo's mad dash through the woods, he passed within sight of David Freeman, who was still bound to a tree and unaware of what had transpired. Freeman yelled, "Nick, help me!" There was no reply from Fiorillo, who just kept running, hell-bent on escaping and getting help.

More alarmed than ever, Freeman worked desperately to free himself. Within five minutes he managed to get loose, and headed immediately in the direction where Carol and Phil were tied. Though he was unarmed, he had to risk saving his friends. He could only hope the stranger had already left the woods.

Approaching the site, Freeman slunk low to the ground to avoid detection. Soon he saw the stranger, holding his rifle and squatting by the tree near Domblewski.

Almost simultaneously, the man spotted Freeman, who realized he was trapped. "Hold it," barked the man. Freeman had no choice but to surrender. He stood up and raised his hands in the air, pleading for mercy and promising to comply with any demands.

The man rose, walked over to Freeman, and said, "You'd better hope your buddy didn't go for help, or you're in trouble. You'd better get him back, or this is it for you. Start calling your friend." He apparently had heard Fiorillo escape after all, but was so engrossed in dealing with Domblewski that he failed to, or was unable to, react.

Freeman started yelling repeatedly for Nick to come back. At gunpoint, the man directed him towards the road to begin searching for Fiorillo.

Unknown to David Freeman, Carol was still tied to a tree, unharmed, and had witnessed his capture by the stranger. As the two men moved off and began looking for Fiorillo, Malinowski debated what to do next.

If she managed to get free and the stranger found her, she had no idea what the consequences might be. Briefly, there was a fear of getting untied, opposed by the fear of remaining bound.

At that point, nobody was aware of Domblewski's condition. He had clearly suffered some type of abuse, perhaps being punched or beaten. Still, it remained possible the man's intent was to tie them up, steal some gas, and flee the area. Should she stay put?

Finally, the urge to escape became irrepressible, as it had been for Fiorillo and Freeman. Carol began to work on her ropes. The tightness of the restraints made it seem impossible, but a bit of quick thinking produced a solution. Digging in with her heels and pushing against the tree, Carol wriggled herself to a standing position. As her hands neared the narrower section of trunk, the ropes slackened somewhat.

In another few minutes she was free of her bonds. Grabbing her purse, rope, and sandals, Malinowski ran towards Domblewski to see if he was okay.

She found her friend still leaning with his back against the tree, and his arms behind the trunk. Touching him on the shoulder to get his attention, Carol suddenly realized Domblewski was covered with blood.

The horrifying reality struck Malinowski that this was no simple gas theft. They had hoped against hope that things would turn out okay, but now she knew they were all in a life-or-death situation.

Other than go for help, there was nothing she could do for Phil, who appeared to be dead. Freeman and Fiorillo were still out there somewhere, and in more danger than perhaps even they realized.

With that in mind, Carol struck out for the road, avoiding the direction taken by the stranger and Freeman in their search for Fiorillo. Without a map and compass, it was notoriously easy to become lost in the thick summer woods, but she had to take that chance.

As Malinowski made her way through the forest, David Freeman, with a loaded rifle trained on him, was still searching for Nick. To offset the man's warnings of what might happen if he didn't find Fiorillo, Freeman repeatedly claimed Nick was hiding somewhere, waiting for him.

Together they walked the route down towards the campsite, where Freeman was marched up and down the roadside, searching persistently but finding nothing. The man directed him up a dirt road for about a half mile, but with still no sign of Nick, they began making their way back towards the highway.

Searching the dirt road was an interesting development. Either the stranger hoped to find Fiorillo's car nearby, or he hadn't noticed earlier that Nick's vehicle was missing from the tent area.

Wondering what fate might await him and his friends, Freeman attempted diversionary tactics. He offered repeated assurances of cooperation, and insisted Fiorillo was somewhere nearby, still scared and hiding. The man's only response was the same one he repeated earlier: "Be quiet and keep walking."

At one point, Freeman noticed the man still wore the knife sheath on his belt, but it was now empty. Maybe he had set the knife down somewhere after cutting a piece of rope and had simply forgotten to pick it up. At any rate, it was one less weapon for Freeman to worry about.

Following the dirt road, and occasionally probing the forest for any sign of Fiorillo, they made their way back towards the blacktopped highway. Finally, the two men arrived at the campsite, where they entered Carol's car. The stranger sat in the back seat, training the rifle on his captive.

Following orders, Freeman drove to the dirt road they had just walked. After proceeding slowly for about a mile, there was still no sign of Nick.

They returned to Old Route 8 and drove to a clearing where

the man's orange Volkswagen Fastback was parked. Once there, David was forced to make another attempt at finding Fiorillo in the woods, but to no avail.

Both men then got into the Volkswagen, again with the man in the back seat, his rifle pointed towards Freeman. David was in danger every moment while held captive, but the incessant search was serving one important purpose: at least it was keeping him alive.

For a third time, they drove past the campsite and accessed the same dirt road, searching all the while for Fiorillo. Nearly a mile up the road, the car began to sputter as if it was running out of gas.

Freeman was instructed to drive into a brushy area. A stump blocked the opening, so he exited the car, moved the stump, and then nosed the vehicle in as far as possible. Next came a command to get out of the car, and with that, the anxiety of the moment skyrocketed.

So far, he had been buying time, hoping that Fiorillo had succeeded in finding help. Had the stranger finally lost patience with the search? Was this the end, the place where he was going to die?

Instead, Freeman was marched once again back to the camping area. Three times they had traveled part of Fly Creek Road and found nothing, but this trip ended differently. As they approached the tent site, his captor seemed to suddenly realize that Fiorillo's car had been missing all along. The kid had escaped!

The man now acted with urgency. They retrieved Carol's car and parked it in the original position near the tent, presenting the appearance that it hadn't been moved. Fiorillo was sure to return, and an undisturbed tent site would indicate everyone was still tied up in the woods, waiting to be rescued.

In preparation for that moment, the man forced Freeman to accompany him across the road, where they took cover in a ditch about six feet deep. There, the watch began. When Nick arrived, the stranger planned to ambush his quarry and regain control of the campers.

The extensive search by Freeman had taken more than

an hour. In the meantime, Fiorillo was trying to get help. After the mad sprint through the woods, he had run to his car and taken off in the direction of Wells. Stopping some motorists, he asked how to contact the police. They told him to go to a Wells restaurant and ask for a man named John.

Fiorillo reached the village at about 10:00 a.m. The man he sought was John Vodron, owner of Vodron's Restaurant. Nick frantically told him what had occurred, at the same time working on removing the rope that was still tied to one of his wrists.

The state police in Fonda, thirty-nine miles south, were notified. Fiorillo was instructed to wait at the restaurant for the arrival of police officers, at which time he would lead them to the scene.

Then, John Vodron sprang into action, accompanied by friend and restaurant patron Kenneth Sherwood. Together they raced off, stopping at the home of Edgar Beaudin, a Hamilton County Highway Department employee. They asked for his assistance, explaining to Beaudin where they were going, and why. With a promise that he would join them soon, the two men headed for the scene.

Vodron and Sherwood scanned the area from Coon Creek Bridge at the south end of Old Route 8 to the bridge at the north end. Finding nothing, they reversed course and encountered Beaudin at the entrance to Robbs Creek Road, an unpaved lane used for logging.

Unable to locate the site in the woods as described by Fiorillo, the three men discussed the possibilities of where the attack might have taken place. After searching the area for tire tracks and finding nothing, they drove to the camping area at Fly Creek Road, where a single tent was still standing.

As he parked on the side of the road, Beaudin noticed a few other cars there besides his and John Vodron's. Though he didn't know it at the time, inside one of those vehicles sat another victim of the abduction, Carol Malinowski.

Carol, after removing her bonds and finding Domblewski soaked with blood, had worked her way through the woods and reached the main highway. Eventually, she was picked up by two young men who took her to a gas station in Speculator.

There, she placed a phone call to the sheriff's office at Lake Pleasant and pleaded for help. Soon after, lawmen picked up Carol and drove to the scene. She waited in the car while the men reviewed her story and decided what action to take.

Unbeknownst to everyone, all of this movement was observed by the stranger and David Freeman, who were lying in a ditch just down the road from the cars. A few minutes earlier, the man had ejected a shell from his rifle and then reloaded it, making certain he was ready for action. Freeman knew he was poised to kill.

Beaudin, Sherwood, and Vodron exited their cars and spoke with the other men at the scene. Edgar Beaudin, finding the conversation somewhat confusing, left the group and stood by his jeep. He was joined there by Ken Sherwood.

As the two of them discussed the situation, they noticed some trampled grass leading towards the woods. Walking to the shoulder of the road for a closer look, they saw nothing at first. Then, turning away abruptly, Beaudin lowered his voice, telling Sherwood there was a man lying down in the ditch.

Ken Sherwood, an experienced woodsman and a licensed New York State guide, stood about ten feet from Beaudin. His perspective revealed nothing unusual, so he took a couple of steps down the bank for a closer look.

The stranger, who had been awaiting the return of Nick Fiorillo, now faced the specter of dealing with several armed men. Realizing he was badly outnumbered, and with his position exposed by Beaudin and Sherwood, escape seemed the only option.

When he suddenly moved towards the woods, all hell broke loose. David Freeman burst from cover and attempted to leap the ditch. In doing so, he stumbled and fell at Sherwood's feet. Rolling onto his back, Freeman shouted warnings that a man with a gun was going to kill them.

Several men instantly ducked behind the cars for protection, while Ken Sherwood turned his attention back to the ditch. Moving hurriedly towards the woods was a man carrying a firearm. Amid the briefly chaotic scene, the stranger vanished into the forest.

Working his way to a sheriff's car parked down the road, Freeman found Carol Malinowksi inside, safe and sound. Together, they shared an emotional reunion.

Ken Sherwood, meanwhile, was prepared to follow the man's trail. Before doing so, he crossed the road to ask Freeman what type of gun the man was carrying. Freeman said he thought it was a .22, a small-bore rifle usually used for small-game hunting and target practice.

One of the men was holding a .30-06, a high-powered, big-game hunting weapon capable of dropping a moose. Sherwood borrowed a shell and showed it to Freeman, who confirmed that it closely resembled the ammo carried by the stranger.

Since the man was heavily armed and clearly dangerous, the decision was made to seal off the area and wait for police to arrive. Pursuit in the heavy brush might make them easy marks for a desperate killer.

By then, several other locals had joined the scene and offered assistance. Immediately they began securing the site by posting men at every outlet. Routes 8 and 30 run together as the main artery east of Speculator, and off that highway and Old Route 8 were several dirt roads used for logging or wilderness camp access.

The men, many of them hunters, were very familiar with the territory. Fanning out across the area, they set up roadblocks at every possible escape route.

With all roads effectively secured by 11:00 a.m., David Freeman and Carol Malinowski were taken to Speculator, and then south a few miles to Lake Pleasant, site of the Hamilton County Jail. There they were questioned at length to find out exactly what had occurred.

In the meantime, Nick Fiorillo's long, tortuous wait at Wells had finally come to an end. New York State Police Lieutenant Michael Halloran arrived at around 11:00 a.m., accompanied by Investigator Arthur Brown and Dr. Charles Woerner.

After an hour of intense anxiety over the fate of his friends, Fiorillo joined the men in the squad car, giving directions north to the campsite. From there, they hiked into the woods to where the four campers had been restrained.

A sad, terrible scene awaited them. Nick found his friend, Philip Domblewski, seated against the tree with his head bowed down towards the ground, dead. His clothing was drenched in blood. A knife protruded from the ground a few feet away.

Alarmingly, there was no sign of Freeman or Malinowski. What had become of them?

Fiorillo stood off to the side while the men examined the scene. When they returned to the police cruiser, he went over the details of the morning's events. Soon, a priest arrived. Nick was asked to guide him to Domblewski's location.

They began to walk through the woods, but a haunting fear quickly overwhelmed Fiorillo. An officer was assigned to accompany them, and when they reached the site, the priest administered the last rites to Domblewski. They returned to the highway in silence.

With the knowledge that a murder had been committed, and that the perpetrator was armed, dangerous, and on the run, more help was needed. The remote site had insufficient radio transmission, so Lieutenant Halloran dispatched Investigator Brown to Lake Pleasant. Brown's job was to summon the necessary manpower, including a crime scene photographer and other investigators. A killer was on the loose, and as far as they knew, he had two hostages with him.

Brown drove to Speculator village, and after contacting the police station in Fonda, he returned to the scene. Nick Fiorillo, who was just emerging from the woods, then accompanied Brown on the drive to Lake Pleasant, where he would give the police an official accounting of events.

When the two men arrived at the Hamilton County Jail, they found Freeman and Malinowski safely in the custody of sheriff's deputies. Brown immediately notified headquarters that all the campers had been accounted for, and that the object of the search was a lone gunman.

Troopers soon began arriving at the scene. Many of them had been involved in the search for Susan Petz, which was still ongoing, though it had been scaled back somewhat. It quickly became clear to investigators that the Domblewski murder paralleled the Daniel Porter case, including several vital details that would not be released to the media. It appeared certain that both crimes had been committed by the same person.

At the Hamilton County Courthouse, Fiorillo, Freeman, and Malinowski were answering dozens of questions posed by investigators. They were shown mug shots of several criminals, and it wasn't long before they had a name: Robert Francis Garrow.

They didn't know it at the time, but the man they were searching for was no ordinary criminal. He would soon become the focal point of one of the most infamous crime sagas in New York State history.

2

Manhunt

Robert Francis Garrow was already a wanted man, and a man with a criminal record. A Syracuse resident for the past five years, he had spent the better part of the 1960s in New York State's maximum-security prisons.

In a violent attack in 1961, Garrow used a pellet gun to knock an Albany area high school football player unconscious, and then raped his girlfriend. The conviction earned him a ten- to twenty-year prison term. He was released on parole in 1968.

Just two months prior to the attack near Speculator, Garrow again found himself in serious legal trouble. Two young girls, ages ten and eleven, were abducted from the Syracuse suburb of Geddes. Their captor took them to a remote location, forcing one girl to masturbate him, and the other to perform oral sex.

A few days after that incident was reported, evidence led police to Garrow, who was arrested on child molestation charges. Despite his record, including several years in prison for violent assault and rape, Garrow was released to his parole officer, due in large part to the efforts of attorney Frank Armani. A court date was set for July 12, just under a month later.

Consequently, a very dangerous man, well known to the criminal justice system, was allowed to roam free for four weeks while awaiting his next court appearance. And when July 12 arrived, Robert Garrow was nowhere to be found.

A postponement court date of July 26 was set, allowing him two more weeks of freedom, but again, Garrow didn't show. At that point, Onondaga County Judge Ormand Gale issued a bench warrant for his arrest on charges of sodomy, sexual abuse, attempted rape, unlawful imprisonment, criminal impersonation, possession of a weapon, and endangering the welfare of a child. The warrant was issued on Friday, July 27. The attack on Domblewski and his friends came just two days later.

Police well knew that the man they were searching for was dangerous. He had brutally slain a helpless captive, was carrying a high-powered rifle, and was on the run. He was also desperate. As the three surviving campers reported, Garrow himself said he had killed before and would kill again.

As the story broke and details emerged, the consistencies between the Porter and Domblewski killings were obvious to police and the public. Both victims were young, long-haired men; both had been stabbed to death in the chest; and both murders occurred within thirty miles of each other in an area where violent crime was virtually nonexistent.

Police confirmed that the two homicides had marked similarities, but officially, there was no physical evidence and no information tying the two together. To aid the ongoing investigation, some of the more intimate details of the attacks were withheld from the media.

Despite the parallels, the second incident was far different from the first in one vital respect. This time there was plenty of evidence. Three potential murder victims had escaped, and they all had information for police to use in identifying their assailant.

The prospects seemed bright for a speedy resolution. Within hours of Domblewski's murder, police knew the identity of the killer. They also knew that he was driving an orange Volkswagen Fastback. Roads had been quickly sealed off after the attack, and bulletins were issued to surrounding law enforcement officers. They were certain the suspect was still somewhere within the general vicinity of the crime scene. A quick capture appeared possible, if not likely.

Garrow, in the meantime, was on the move. After narrowly escaping the campsite encounter, he worked his way through the thick woods along Fly Creek Road and located the Volkswagen where he and Freeman had left it earlier.

Though it had begun to sputter at the time, it was not out of fuel after all. Managing to get it started, he drove deeper into the woods, searching for a possible way out. Soon he met another vehicle, a Cadillac, headed towards the paved highway.

The two cars slowed to a crawl as they passed each other. The woman driving the Cadillac looked at the occupant of the Volkswagen and was greeted with a smile and a nod. She nearly stopped to visit, thinking the man's friendly greeting indicated he knew her husband. But the smaller car kept moving, so the woman continued on her way.

When she reached the end of Fly Creek Road at about 11:30 a.m., mayhem ensued. The driver of the Cadillac, Jan Mary Tracy, had just left her camp, but found access to Old Route 8 was blocked. At the intersection sat a truck, flanked by two men wielding rifles.

When the order came to get out of her car, Tracy screamed, dropped the vehicle into reverse, and roared backwards up the hillside, all the while blowing the horn. After about a quarter mile, she finally lost control and ended up in a ditch.

Unable to free the car, she grabbed the keys and her purse and continued up the road for more than half a mile, running and screaming for help until she finally reached the camp.

It was fortunate that Mrs. Tracy didn't meet the stranger again as she ran up the roadway. Ironically, she was fleeing from safety into potential danger, where a deadly killer lurked. Garrow, however, was busy searching for a way to escape the woods road. He eventually discovered that the only way out was back to Old Route 8.

Within a few hours of Domblewski's murder, lawmen were rushing to the scene in substantial numbers. More than a hundred police officers busied themselves establishing a network of roadblocks and developing a search strategy. Officials felt sure they had the suspect hemmed in, and that it was only a matter of time before he would give himself up. By nightfall, however, he was still on the loose.

Unbeknownst to the troopers, Garrow had hidden his car off Fly Creek Road and covered it with tree branches. His strategy was to sit tight as searchers prowled the highways and back roads, looking for any sign of him. As darkness enveloped the mountains, the chances of police finding him were greatly diminished.

Troopers searching at night would need to use lighting, making any officer an all-too-easy target for a man with a high-powered rifle. Police were forced to play an intense, nerve-wracking waiting game, hoping their quarry would reveal himself, or simply surrender.

It was well past midnight when Garrow decided to make his move. Under cover of darkness, he drove the Volkswagen down Fly Creek Road towards the highway, accelerating as he neared the end of the dirt road. The tires enjoyed a much better grip on the macadam surface as Garrow turned south and gunned the engine, pushing the little VW for all it was worth.

As he exited the dirt road, the lights of a police cruiser burst into view in his rearview mirror. Trooper Michael Kelleher, the guard posted at the end of Fly Creek Road that night, had been sitting with a partner in an unlit patrol car, watching for any sign of the fugitive. He observed the fast-moving car, with branches dangling from it, as it careened onto the highway.

Notifying the command post, Kelleher began pursuit, and a wild, high-speed chase ensued. Though Garrow had the advantage of a head start, both he and the police officers knew that a Volkswagen could not outrun a patrol car.

The powerful engine of the troopers' vehicle would surely overtake the smaller car within a minute or so. If nothing else, Garrow expected he would soon encounter a roadblock.

Kelleher gained ground quickly despite the initial disadvantage, but entering a series of curves presented an opportunity for Garrow, prompting a quick decision. With the patrol car momentarily out of sight, he swerved from the main highway, detouring into a brushy area.

As the troop car emerged from the curves, nothing but darkness loomed ahead. The speeding car had vanished.

Continuing down the highway, Kelleher neared a sharp curve, and suddenly slammed his foot down on the brake pedal. Something had caught his eye, and as he backed up the patrol car, there it was. The tiny Volkswagen slowly came into view, facing Kelleher. A glint from the car's windshield had given up its location.

The intense chase had lasted just under a mile, and it now appeared that Kelleher had his man. He again radioed the command post, updating the situation. Then, with his spotlight on the vehicle parked about seventy-five feet from the paved highway, he ordered the occupant to come forward and surrender. There was no response.

The tension heightened, and Kelleher's adrenaline raced. He knew the man was armed, and the bright spotlight presented an inviting target. But the officer's repeated commands to come forward were met with silence, and it was finally determined that Garrow was not present after all.

Grabbing his rifle and other gear, he had quickly left the car and blended into the night woods. For the officers, any attempt at pursuit in those conditions was foolhardy, if not suicidal. Flashlights would transform the hunters themselves into easy prey for a killer on the loose.

Police searched Garrow's vehicle, and among the items reportedly found was a road map with markings on it. Across the northern New York region were twenty-seven dots in red ink, with female first names appearing near several of them.

The effect was sobering. Officials realized they might be on to something much bigger than first suspected. The dots suggested the frightening possibility that each one represented another victim of rape or murder. It was now more important than ever to bring this man in, and to bring him in alive. Besides his known crimes, he may hold the key to solving many others.

Garrow was still free, but police were now certain he hadn't wandered miles through the woods and escaped the region. With knowledge of where the suspect was located, the resources of the law were concentrated in an area known to locals as Coon Creek, where Garrow's car had been abandoned.

When daylight arrived, the search intensified, utilizing bloodhounds, two New York State police helicopters, and about 140 state troopers. Unlike the difficulties officials faced in the search for Susan Petz, this time the bloodhounds and helicopters seemed to have a good chance of finding their quarry.

In the case of Petz, police didn't know if there was any type of trail for the bloodhounds to pick up. And, in that location, there were few opportunities to spot anything from above due to the dense leaf cover in the surrounding woods.

With Garrow, they knew who they were after, and they knew where he had entered the forest. They also had his car and some personal belongings left in it, providing plenty of scent for the bloodhounds to begin the hunt.

The forest where the helicopters were searching was very thick, but there were several natural clearings that required monitoring. Most importantly, in the vast wooded area north and east of Speculator, there was an extensive network of trails, logging roads, and camp roads. All afforded opportunities to spot the fugitive.

Of course, Garrow was likely bushwhacking (hiking without using trails) to avoid detection, but that tactic can be especially demoralizing in thick forest cover. The summer heat and the intense biting insects that torment all living creatures entering their domain worsened the conditions.

For most people, virtually any type of road or trail is preferable to bushwhacking. It was hoped that Garrow might choose an established path for speed of movement, opening himself to aerial exposure.

Beginning at the abandoned car, bloodhounds followed the scent, and at around 9:00 a.m. they discovered a binoculars case and a red bag dropped by the fugitive as he fled into the woods on the previous night. The location of the items reaffirmed officials' belief that Garrow remained in the Fly Creek–Robbs Creek area.

As the search continued on Monday, details began to surface about the subject of the manhunt. Newspapers across the state picked up the stories, and readers everywhere learned of Garrow's past problems with the law. The assault and rape convictions in Albany, plus the years of hard time in maximum-security prisons at Dannemora and Auburn, made the headlines.

As reporters probed deeper, more facts were revealed. In November 1972, Garrow had been charged with unlawful imprisonment and possession of a dangerous drug. The charges stemmed from an incident involving two hitchhikers, Syracuse University students Leonard Garner and Karen Lutz. After a harrowing midnight ride, they had managed to escape.

The pair subsequently accused Garrow of holding them hostage at gunpoint and tying them up. The drug charges pertained to a small bag of marijuana found underneath the back seat of his car.

Garrow's attorney, Frank Armani of Syracuse, eventually determined that the drugs actually belonged to the students. When the case went to court for resolution, the pair declined to press charges, prompting a rebuke from the judge, along with some unfortunate commentary.

He lauded Garrow's fine record since being released from prison, noting that past transgressions did not carry an automatic presumption of guilt on future charges. In setting the defendant free, the judge proclaimed he was "righting a miscarriage of justice against Robert Garrow." Those were words he would live to regret.

There were other blights on Garrow's record. The most ominous, of course, was the recent abduction and molestation of the two young girls from Geddes. And now, there were new charges. Hamilton County District Attorney William Intemann, Jr., announced he was preparing a warrant for Garrow's arrest on charges of first-degree murder in the death of Philip Domblewski.

As more revelations were made in newspapers across New York, the search by helicopters, bloodhounds, and nearly 150 law officers continued to come up empty. When darkness fell on Monday evening, it became clear that nobody was going home just yet.

Despite the seemingly overwhelming odds against him, Robert Garrow actually held an advantage. At about 2:00 a.m. on Monday, he had left his vehicle behind and taken to the woods. The dense Adirondack forest wasn't exactly home, but he was much more familiar with his surroundings than were most of the searchers. Until the age of fifteen, he had grown up in the Mineville-Witherbee area in northern New York State, a rugged, mountainous region near Lake Champlain's western shore.

Mineville's cornerstone industry closed in 1971 after producing some of the nation's best iron ore for more than a century. Like just about everyone else in town, Garrow's father had been a mine employee. It was an extremely tough life, and miners' families relied on hunting and fishing to provide some of life's essentials. Most male family members became closely acquainted with the nuances of surviving and navigating in the woods. Those skills were as much a necessity as they were a pastime.

That was Robert Garrow's background, and now it served him well. He wasn't an expert woodsman, but a familiarity with the Adirondack terrain, combined with a strong urge not to be found, clearly worked in his favor. Those factors alone could make it very difficult to capture him. Two days of searching had already proven fruitless.

Though he was not aware of it, there was another element working in his favor. The order had been given to capture Garrow alive if at all possible. Even if he was sighted at a distance, firearms were not to be used to disable him unless lives were in immediate danger.

The story of Garrow's abduction of the four campers had spread across the state, capturing the attention of radio, television, and newspapers. In the Adirondack region, it was the topic of conversation at every diner, restaurant, store, and barbershop. The terrorizing of his victims, the vicious murder, the wild escape, and the subsequent manhunt all made for a tale that was absolutely gripping.

Besides interest, the story sparked fear. Newspapers committed their resources to covering the unfolding drama, frequently recounting Garrow's past crimes, plus the fact that he was armed and dangerous. People were made aware, and the more they knew, the more scared they became. Many shuddered to think what other crimes Garrow might have committed.

The fear spread, and it soon permeated the Adirondacks, a once peaceful haven. Doors that had gone unlocked for decades were now bolted and barricaded. Old guns were dusted off, new guns were purchased, and ammo sales soared.

Rifles and shotguns were kept by the bedside, and pistols were at arm's reach. Housewives, sons, and daughters were taught how to use firearms. The impact on North Country life cannot be overstated.

It was then revealed that, on July 27, just two days prior to the Domblewski murder, Garrow had been seen at Camp of the Woods, a Christian retreat center located on the northeast shore of Lake Pleasant in Speculator. He had attempted to block a young woman from entering her cabin, but she managed to escape the frightening confrontation unscathed.

The next morning, Saturday, July 28, two young girls were riding their bicycles in front of Camp of the Woods. A man with a rifle had tried to stop them and take their bicycles, but the girls rode away from him.

It was barely twenty-four hours later and a few miles away that Garrow attacked the four campers and murdered Philip Domblewski. Considering his past crimes, it was very likely the three young people at Camp of the Woods had narrowly escaped a horrible fate.

As the manhunt continued, the likelihood increased that a reliable tip from a civilian would bring Garrow in. There had been several such calls on Monday, the day after Domblewski was killed.

On Tuesday a flood of information began to arrive, and two more phone lines were installed at the police command post to handle the volume. (This was 1973, when prototypes of portable telephones were only in the early testing stages, and three decades before cell phones would become commonplace.)

In one call that spurred hope, a helicopter was dispatched to look for a suspicious man reportedly seen near an area camp. Tensions ran high, but the search produced nothing. There was hardly time for disappointment, though, as dozens of supposed sightings kept officers busy.

Several other contacts received by police involved camp break-ins, which are routine occurrences in the Adirondacks. Camps are often in remote locations, visited infrequently by owners and only occasionally by hired caretakers. They are regularly targeted by burglars.

Each such incident now took on added significance with Garrow on the loose. There was an expectation that he would be seeking food, clothing, weapons, and personal items. Backwoods camps were the obvious source of supply.

On Tuesday, July 31, at least four camp break-ins were reported in the vicinity of Speculator. Each time, anxiety intensified as troopers were dispatched to the scene, facing potentially deadly consequences. Some of the burglaries were attributed to Garrow based on the types of items that were stolen. So far, though, there was no irrefutable evidence at any of the camps to indicate he had been present.

An abandoned car bearing Vermont license plates was reported near the Warren-Hamilton County line, causing alarm among nearby residents. Eventually it was determined that the car belonged to a camper who planned to exit the woods on Thursday. Since the vehicle was within several miles of a recent murder scene, police checked it regularly until the hiker returned safely.

One call came from a woman in South Glens Falls, claiming she had seen a man fitting Garrow's description. Police did not believe he had escaped the Speculator area, but a trooper was dispatched to check out the possible sighting. No lead was allowed to pass without investigation.

Towards evening, police were notified that someone in Newcomb, thirty-three miles north of Speculator, had seen a man stumbling out of the woods. Though it at first seemed unlikely, police calculated that it was possible for Garrow to have walked that far since his disappearance on Monday.

Captain Fred Teeple of the Bureau of Criminal Investigation (BCI) was dispatched to Newcomb to investigate. When police arrived, the man was nowhere to be found. The team, accompanied by a bloodhound, worked until darkness but turned up nothing. For a third day Garrow had managed to avoid capture, and no one knew where he was.

At about 1:20 a.m. Wednesday, police received a call from Northville in Fulton County, about thirty miles south of Speculator on Route 30. It appeared to be the break officials had been hoping for. David C. Burton, 23, claimed that a knife-wielding man had attacked him in an attempt to steal his car. Quickly, a team of twenty armed officers was sent to the scene.

They were greeted by a victim suffering from minor facial wounds. After hearing the man's story and investigating further, police had suspicions about the alleged confrontation. Eventually Burton came clean, admitting there had been no attack at all. He had been injured in a fall from his front porch. He was later found guilty of falsely reporting an incident and sentenced to sixty days in jail.

Police had little to show for their efforts so far, and the multitude of tips and leads had proven more of a hindrance than a help. In one day, Garrow had reportedly been sighted thirty-three miles north of Speculator in Newcomb; thirty-nine miles east in South Glens Falls; and now thirty miles south at Northville. In the press, he began to take on the aura of a slick, elusive killer. Some referred to him as "phantom-like."

But there was no great mystery to staying undetected in the vast woods surrounding Speculator. The wild forest there is dense and expansive. Just one section north of the village, bound by Routes 30, 28, and 8, comprises a rectangle of about 250 square miles. That is the area that Garrow was known to have entered. Just across any of those secluded highways was another huge wilderness.

In the Adirondacks, there are many heavily forested sections with no official hiking trails, but woven throughout the region are thousands of miles of dirt roads, rough logging roads, and footpaths. The open avenues might have been helpful to searchers, but it was now believed Garrow would avoid them. They sometimes offered little canopy cover, and a helicopter crew might be able to spot any movement below.

This difficult landscape required boots on the ground, and it would take a virtual army to cover the area in question. It was still suspected that Garrow was in the vicinity of Robbs Creek and Fly Creek, about four miles northeast of Speculator village.

Unless a person has actually bushwhacked in those woods during the summer, it is hard to imagine what it was like for state police, conservation officers, and sheriff's deputies. As a hiker, if you don't like bushwhacking, then you probably hate it. It is far more punishment than pleasure for most people.

Consider first that searchers were moving about, looking for a dangerous killer who carried a rifle and was doing his best to remain undetected. For the most part, dense vegetation is what these men were dealing with, and dense vegetation comes with its own set of problems.

Progress is very slow, usually less than a third or a quarter of the average trail-hiking speed. Visibility is extremely limited in most circumstances, often reduced to only a few feet. In open woods with more mature tree growth, the sight range can be increased by squatting down below branch level and peering through the forest. In brush or very dense woods, squatting has little or no effect.

The thick summer foliage holds another powerful deterrent to woods travel: insects. Most of the bugs in the Adirondacks are no problem, but when they are of the biting variety, it doesn't take many small insects to present a huge hindrance and make life downright miserable.

Black flies are perhaps the most infamous bugs in the Adirondacks. Some are constantly annoying, swarming wildly about the head and face, while the biting versions attack aggressively. They come in many sizes and maintain continuous harassment, which can be incredibly discouraging to anyone in the woods.

In this particular case, the normal black fly season of May and June was well past, but as many hikers will attest, there seems to be some type of black fly producing hatches of hungry hordes all summer long.

At the time of the Garrow manhunt, mosquitoes were in full attack mode. To be bothered by even a few mosquitoes at one time is a nuisance. Searchers in the summer forest faced something entirely different, a creature that attacked in numbers, relentlessly probing through clothing, skin, and insect repellant.

Besides mosquitoes, deer flies are among the worst of the insect pests. In the summer woods, swarms of a half-dozen or more deer flies are often seen buzzing interminably around the heads of poor, beleaguered hikers. The noise itself is annoying, but sudden quiet might be a sign of something worse. The tormentor has probably landed, and is about to give a nasty bite as it feasts on the host's blood.

Another hazard of bushwhacking is heat. The enclosed forest

is generally cool early in the morning, but once the warmth of July or August percolates throughout the day, the effect becomes stifling. Constant movement can be energy-sapping.

Imagine, then, the effects of such a demoralizing confluence of afflictions. Oppressive heat; long shifts of twelve to twenty-four hours; constant assault by deer flies, mosquitoes, and black flies; leaves and branches slapping against the face and body; profuse sweating; odoriferous insect repellant; and aching feet from spending day after day in the rough Adirondack woods.

Add to that a dangerous killer perhaps lurking behind the next tree or just over the rise, and you have an idea of what searchers for Garrow experienced. The Adirondacks truly are a wonderful place in many ways, but the untamed areas are not for the weak-willed. Choosing to face such obstacles is one thing, but being thrust into the situation is another thing entirely.

The best that searchers could do was wear long-sleeved shirts and long pants to ward off the bushes and bugs, though such clothing intensified the effects of the heat. Insect repellant was used liberally, its effectiveness reduced by constant sweating, which served to rinse the chemicals from any exposed skin.

The only good solution to all of the discomfort and danger was to capture Robert Garrow.

As the manhunt entered its fourth day, officials had established a solid network of roadblocks across the region. In the immediate area of Speculator, barricades were positioned every few miles. Each stop involved a quick but complete vehicle search, including the trunk.

In the 1970s, few automobiles featured convenient, in-car trunk releases. At every roadblock, the driver had to shut the ignition off, exit the vehicle, and unlock the trunk. What began as a minor inconvenience soon became a major annoyance, and then a dreaded encounter.

Locals suffered the consequences, enduring eight to ten searches on a round-trip drive between neighboring communities like Speculator and Wells. The roadblocks spanned three counties, affecting everyone across the region at some level.

In the woods, four bloodhounds constantly prowled for any sign of Garrow. When police searched a particular area, heavily armed foot patrols and vehicles maintained the perimeter, while a wave of officers entered the designated grid and combed the forest.

Keeping the fugitive on the move increased the chances he would be seen by someone, which was far less likely were he allowed to just sit tight and wait. Authorities hoped that either hunger or the relentless swarms of insects would induce Garrow to finally give up.

In the interests of public safety, police evacuated campers from the area. That in itself was no small accomplishment. August in Speculator usually attracted a thousand or more campers to the region. Some preferred lakeside locations near the village, but many sought the solitude of remote sites miles deep into the wilderness. (In those days, the term "campers" referred mainly to people who stayed in tents. Motorized camping was yet to become commonplace.)

A number of campers had already vacated the area late Sunday, which was normal procedure in the Adirondacks, as visitors returned home from a weekend in the mountains. Others left of their own volition due to the potential danger from Garrow, and from the great number of armed men present in the woods, which increased the chance of some type of accident. Any remaining campers were warned to leave for their own safety.

All visitors to the area were discouraged from canoeing the Sacandaga River near Speculator, and especially the trip on the Kunjamuk River, a small stream that connects the Sacandaga to Elm Lake. Those favored sites were in the vicinity of where Garrow was believed to be hiding.

It was critical to protect citizens who might be in danger. Even as heavy rain hit the area on Tuesday night, searchers continued working, checking on hundreds of campsites in the expansive backwoods country.

By Wednesday morning, calls began coming in again, and before noon at least ten people had reported Garrow sightings, all in widely scattered locations. Each report had to be checked out by officials before it could be discounted.

A new tactic was added to the search on Wednesday. Helicopters flew back and forth above the area, playing recorded messages begging the fugitive to surrender. Garrow's wife, Edith, and his thirteen-year-old son, Robert, Jr., had come to Speculator on Tuesday to produce the recordings for police.

Mrs. Garrow's voice pleaded, "Honey, this is Edith. Won't you please come, and leave your rifle in the woods?" Young Robert's voice followed with, "We don't want you to get hurt. Please come out." Hour after hour, their appeals rang out from low-flying helicopters, resonating across the hillsides.

Late in the morning, police received important news. A search team member, New York State Trooper Warren Churco, had found a red hunting shirt about twenty feet from a dirt road near Owl Pond. The discovery came as the group returned from checking several remote camps.

Churco had been standing in the back of a pickup truck, leaning over the cab while alertly scanning the passing terrain. As the truck moved slowly along the uneven surface, he noticed a patch of red on the ground about halfway between the pond and the road.

Churco's find was significant. The shirt appeared to have been discarded recently, and Garrow was wearing a red shirt when he fled into the woods near Coon Creek on Monday. If it was indeed his, it meant the suspect had wandered seven miles deep into the forest directly north of Speculator village, and seven miles northwest of the current search focus near Coon Creek.

By any measure, that's a long walk in the dense woods. But Garrow was on the run, and likely didn't know how far his pursuers would follow after he eluded police on Monday morning. Since then, he certainly had plenty of time to reach Owl Pond, which also afforded him several opportunities along the way to raid remote camps for food and clothing.

Locals who knew the woods north of Speculator were aware that Fly Creek Road, via three deep-woods intersections, gave direct access to the shores of Owl Pond. Garrow could have used the roadways for easy, speedy travel on the eight-mile walk, ducking for cover at the sound of helicopters. He also might have made the trip under cover of darkness.

Speculation focused on the origins of the shirt and what it

might reveal about the hunted man. At one point it was surmised that Garrow had perhaps deemed the red shirt too visible and may have simply removed it.

However, knowledgeable woodsmen, familiar with the protection shirts provide against biting bugs, whipping branches, and the nighttime cold, concluded Garrow abandoned the shirt after obtaining other clothing. In spite of the red shirt's visibility, it was extremely unlikely he had simply discarded it with nothing else to wear for protection.

To verify that the shirt belonged to Garrow, plans were made immediately to bring Edith back to Speculator. In the meantime, the focal point of the search moved to the Owl Pond area, near the center of the vast wilderness to the north between Speculator and Newcomb. Somewhere out there, Robert Francis Garrow still roamed free.

Bloodhounds were put on the scent where the shirt was found, but that effort was foiled by the heavy rain that had fallen nearly the entire night. Up to 175 searchers continued their efforts to find the elusive suspect, but since the brief car chase in the darkness of early Monday morning, he had not been seen for several days.

Besides the molestation charges awaiting him in Syracuse, Garrow now faced additional legal problems. District Attorney Intemann made it official on Tuesday, issuing a warrant charging him with Domblewski's murder. Police also believed Garrow was involved in the Porter killing, along with the disappearance of Susan Petz.

He was now sought for questioning in many other open cases of murder and rape in central and northern New York. Investigators knew that patience was critical. They wanted him in custody, and they needed him alive. Robert Garrow's death could relegate many of those serious crimes to the cold case file, perhaps never to be solved.

Though the constant rain may have helped erase any scent or tracks left by Garrow, it also served another purpose that gave some relief to the beleaguered troopers. With the bad weather, fewer people were out and about, and the number of Garrow sightings called in to the police command post diminished. At least for the time being, there were fewer empty leads taking officers away from the Speculator area.

Still, the job before searchers was daunting. For days it was believed that Garrow was in the vicinity of Robbs Creek, not far from where he had abandoned his car. But now, if Edith could confirm that the red shirt was her husband's, he had actually traveled several miles from Robbs Creek, and was probably somewhere within a 250-square-mile section of wild forest.

The keyword was probably. If Garrow had continued north or west without being detected, it was anybody's guess how long he might elude police, or if he would be caught at all.

On Wednesday it came to light that a battle was brewing over Garrow in Onondaga County. District Attorney Leo F. Hayes had issued a subpoena to obtain his parole records, and a problem had arisen. Such records included psychiatric test results and other information considered confidential.

Due to the nature and severity of his earlier crimes, Hayes felt Garrow should have been held in jail until the charges had been investigated thoroughly. Instead, he had been released on bail, and his parole status had been maintained.

Further complicating matters, Garrow never showed for his court dates, and now was suspected of murdering Porter and Domblewski, and possibly Susan Petz, in the interim. If an official along the way was determined to have "dropped the ball," the repercussions could be very damaging. It appeared that Garrow had conducted a reign of terror during the very time he could have, or should have, been in jail awaiting court action on the Geddes incident.

As the search in the Adirondacks faded into Wednesday night, information on Garrow was updated to all locations. He had been described earlier as 5 feet 11 inches tall, weighing about 210 to 220 pounds, husky, brown-haired, blue-eyed, and dangerous. He was wearing a red shirt, and according to the photographs that were disseminated, he wore glasses.

However, it was noted that a pair of glasses, assumed to be Garrow's, had been found in the vicinity of Domblewski's body. Updates suggested that Garrow was likely without his glasses, and probably wearing a different colored shirt.

On Thursday came news from another legal front. US Magistrate Edward M. Conan issued a warrant citing Garrow for violating the federal firearms law. When purchasing a rifle from Sears & Roebuck, Garrow had lied by certifying he had no prior felony convictions. The offense carried a maximum penalty of five years in prison and a $5,000 fine.

More importantly, the federal charge brought agents of the Alcohol, Tobacco, and Firearms Division of the U.S. Treasury into the manhunt. When informed the agents were planning to join the search, BCI Lieutenant John Lawliss said, "With the charges we can place against him, they'll have to wait in line for their crack at him."

Also on Thursday morning, Edith Garrow examined the shirt that searchers had found near Owl Pond. She couldn't guarantee that it belonged to her husband, but believed it was his. The size matched, and she knew he possessed a red hunting shirt like the one found.

With that information, the manhunt pushed forward for a fifth day. Troopers used a methodical grid search in an attempt to close in on their quarry, but since Monday at about 2:00 a.m., there had been no confirmed sightings of Garrow.

Late in the afternoon, everything changed in an instant. A pair of travelers reported seeing Garrow crouched in the woods along Route 8, about two miles east of the junction with Route 30. Incredibly, if the information was accurate, Garrow was now located about eleven miles southeast of the focus of the hunt near Owl Pond. This was a wanted man clearly on the move.

Police were dispatched to the scene, and within fifteen minutes, a report came in: Garrow had indeed been sighted. All the bogus reports of the past five days were suddenly forgotten. This time it was for real.

Troopers Morris and Lepage, the two officers sent to investigate, had observed Garrow near a roadside parking area, with rifle in hand, an estimated thirty or forty yards from them. When Morris yelled, "Freeze, don't move," Garrow rushed back into the woods.

As Lepage quickly went to radio for help, Gary Morris began pursuit of the fugitive, but it soon became clear he would need assistance. Delaying the chase was the only option. Otherwise, he might be doing little more than offering himself as a target.

Garrow was now about twenty miles west of where Daniel Porter was murdered, and five miles southeast of the Domblewski site. With word of the confirmed sighting, one hundred state police officers were dispatched to the new location.

Morris and Lepage provided information that verified earlier suspicions: Garrow was not wearing glasses, and he was now clad in a blue-checkered shirt, not the red one he had originally worn. And he still had his firearm.

The small army of police, sheriff's deputies, and conservation officers swung into action. State troopers quickly formed a line covering a six-mile stretch of Route 8 to prevent Garrow from crossing the highway. Bloodhounds were rushed to the scene, and helicopters hovered above, guiding the search.

At one point, a pilot sighted Garrow, but he disappeared again into the forest cover. The hounds were doing their job, though, and after picking up the scent, they were hot on Garrow's trail. He was on the run, and by all appearances, they would soon have their man.

Then, at about 7:00 p.m., a fierce thunderstorm struck, forcing the helicopters to take refuge on land, and effectively ending any further pursuit of Garrow. Amazingly, he had once again avoided capture.

The intensity of the storm drove troopers to seek cover in their cars along Route 8, but Major Francis Staincamp was quickly on the case. His message to all: "This is the Major. Get out of those goddamned cars and get on the road where you can see the next man in line." The order was as much for their own protection as it was to prevent Garrow from crossing the highway.

The storm lasted for more than an hour, but even with darkness encroaching, the searchers were not allowed to leave the scene. Instead, flashlights, flares, and guns and ammunition were brought in, and the men prepared to maintain their positions through the night. It was hoped that a change in tactics would bring a change in results. Troop commanders wanted to keep Garrow nervous and on the move.

After darkness fell, officers were placed in the woods at listening posts, hoping to hear Garrow moving about. All through the night, heavily armed troopers drove back and forth on the highways, trying to keep the fugitive hemmed in, and hoping to wear him down.

Officials were also busy analyzing new information that might help track their quarry. Between Speculator and Wells, on the stretch of road where Routes 8 and 30 coincide, officers found a series of lean-tos only a short distance from the highway. It was believed Garrow had constructed them as safe havens to avoid the search teams, moving from one to another as needed.

The discovery offered clues to Garrow's movements. Despite the fact that he had traveled long distances since his escape, it was now known that he also spent considerable time along roadways, well within reach of the search team.

The all-night effort yielded nothing new, but early Friday morning, bloodhounds picked up Garrow's scent, and again the chase was on. For a mile and a half, searchers followed the trail. Fresh human feces were found along the way, and the tension mounted as officers closed in on their prey.

Then, the scent ended abruptly on the banks of the Sacandaga River. It became apparent that Garrow had entered the fast-moving stream, foiling the bloodhounds once again.

Later in the day, at about 5:30 p.m., a report came in of another camp burglary. Among the items stolen were peanut butter, crackers, batteries, and a compass. If Garrow was the burglar, a compass would certainly enhance his ability to move about the area. He already knew the main highways in the region, and had gained extensive knowledge about the forested areas during the past week.

And, considering the types of goods stolen, it was a virtual certainty that Garrow was, in fact, the burglar. No local criminal would be interested in such otherwise trivial items.

Police crime-lab technicians were sent to the camp in search of fingerprints or other evidence to confirm Garrow had been present. At the same time, troopers were checking the various lean-tos they had found.

From the sighting on Thursday, they knew Garrow was

armed, and from .30-caliber ammunition found in one of the lean-tos, they knew it was a rifle and not a shotgun that he was carrying. That gave him far greater range and accuracy should he decide at some point to use the weapon against police.

Major Staincamp, leader of the search, also pointed out, "The man has shown considerable endurance running through the woods, away from our searchers." They also believed that he had eaten the crackers and peanut butter, so his physical capabilities probably hadn't faded much.

After the most recent sighting of Garrow, discussions on his appearance and the effectiveness of the search exposed a serious operational flaw. Confusion had occurred when some officers were seen wearing street clothing while on the job.

Though it was more comfortable and suitable for conditions, wearing personal clothing in the woods during the manhunt was simply unwise and unsafe. It was critical that Garrow's appearance remained markedly different from his pursuers.

To avoid mistaken identification among the nearly two hundred searchers, dozens of gray uniforms were brought in and distributed. Upwards of sixty new pairs of shoes were also given to the men to replace worn footwear beaten up from days of traversing the rough mountain terrain.

And it wasn't just the shoes that were suffering. The men were also taking a beating, some more than others. Forest rangers and conservation officers were familiar with the territory and the conditions they encountered, but state police officers made up the bulk of the search teams. Many of them came from city locations and were ill-prepared for what they faced.

One trooper's comments helped put it in perspective: "Back home I don't even walk to the local grocery store. Now, I just finished walking through fifteen miles of swamps. It's quite a change."

Each day they emerged from the woods nursing scratches, welts, and a variety of insect bites. At times it was so bad that many were convinced the relentless bugs would eventually force Garrow to surrender. For the men trailing him, it was one of the worst things they endured.

Still, troopers remained upbeat, and they were encouraged

by the near-capture during Friday morning's pursuit. Tracking him for some distance gave searchers an idea of where Garrow might be spending much of his time. That information, combined with the recent discovery of several rough lean-tos, refocused the hunt on more familiar territory, the section of roadway shared by Routes 8 and 30 east and southeast east of Speculator.

After all the movement of the past five days from Robbs Creek to Owl Pond, and then to Route 8, it appeared that Garrow was right back where he had started five days ago, not far from where he had slain Philip Domblewski.

Police were concerned, and rightly so, about the location of some of Garrow's lean-tos. One was situated within earshot of the roadside command post in a parking area along Route 8. Officials knew there were times when Garrow was listening to them from just inside the forest. This led to the discomforting realization that a rifle-toting fugitive may have been observing their efforts from close range.

Besides the frequent rain and thunderstorms that had caused many setbacks, searchers were also hampered occasionally by fog so thick that it was difficult to see the next officer stationed just down the road. This was a real concern, as police strategy was to maintain man-to-man visual contact so Garrow could not cross the highway undetected. The weather, particularly the dense fog, hindered that phase of the plan.

Unofficial reports circulated that fresh searchers would soon be summoned to offer relief. This was good news, for many of the men were spending twelve hours a day in unfamiliar, difficult circumstances. It was crucial to remember one important fact: the more exhausted the men became, the greater the likelihood that mistakes would occur. Even the smallest of errors in this type of manhunt bore potentially fatal consequences.

On Saturday, August 5, the principal investigators convened a four-hour meeting and reviewed all the evidence gathered during the past six days. In the meantime, the search continued, with police expressing disappointment that Garrow hadn't been captured yet. They believed he was still somewhere in the woods near Speculator. Efforts were concentrated on a triangular area marked by Wells, Speculator, and the Route 8 command post.

Footprints found in the woods were among the evidence indicating that Garrow was still within this 140-square-mile tract of forest. It was deemed important to confine him there for as long as possible. Perhaps hunger, frustration, exhaustion, or the elements might push him to surrender.

One puzzling piece of evidence turned up on Saturday, a fresh set of women's footprints about 130 feet from Route 8, and only a mile from the last sighting of Garrow. A nearby home was vacant, having been evacuated shortly after the slaying. And in the 1970s, there were comparatively few female police officers. With those two possible sources of the footprints largely eliminated, speculation suggested that Susan Petz might still be alive and was being held captive by Garrow.

In an effort to solve the mystery, police were ordered to catalog the footwear of all women passing within the boundaries of the search area. Females were required to remove their shoes so officers could record tread details and other information, adding a further annoyance for local residents who traveled back and forth through the roadblocks.

There were now upwards of two hundred search team members looking for Garrow, all of them paid officers. Police made it clear they were not seeking volunteers to help with the manhunt. Tourists and visitors were urged to avoid the area if at all possible. The presence of gawkers would only complicate their efforts and place more people in potential danger. State officials further reduced the amount of traffic by banning all camping in the Wells-Speculator region.

The hunt for Garrow caused much excitement and concern across the Adirondacks, but the effect on Speculator was the most dramatic. Each August a few thousand people flocked to the tiny resort village for sun, fun, and relaxation. Most year-round residents earned the bulk of their annual incomes from the influx of summer tourists. Now motels were filled with state troopers, and the resort atmosphere was largely absent.

Some business owners were not happy with the situation. At one local establishment, troopers returned from a twelve-hour shift only to find their belongings removed and the rooms rented to travelers. It was an unusual occurrence, however, since motels were among the businesses least damaged financially by the effects of the manhunt.

Expenditures on basics like food and gas lagged somewhat, but other parts of the local economy took a more drastic hit. Unlike tourists, searchers were not shopping for luxuries or visiting area attractions. Those two factors were, and are, critical to the survival of most Adirondack villages, and it was those businesses that suffered the most.

Wells also felt the impact dramatically. Among other things, the search for Garrow led to cancellation of their annual festival, the year's most important fundraising and social event.

Near Speculator, some people voiced displeasure with the disruption the manhunt brought to their lives. Most, though, decided to make the best of a bad situation, realizing that things wouldn't change until the killer was captured. They understood that most of the troopers were family men, suddenly uprooted from their lives and saddled with a job that was frustrating, disheartening, and dangerous.

The men were doing their best to capture Garrow alive, and at the same time protect the public. An armed officer even rode the school bus traveling the back roads each day, bringing local youngsters to the village for participation in youth programs. A police vehicle followed the bus as an added precaution.

Despite the great inconvenience of numerous roadblocks and the presence of two hundred armed officers in their usually quiet community, a number of area residents responded to the situation with kindness. A local service station owner extended shop hours, and even gave a pump key to the officer in charge, ensuring uninterrupted fuel access for the fleet of police vehicles.

People from Wells collected money to buy personal items that the searchers lacked. Some made daily trips to the roadblocks, their cars laden with cookies, soda, sandwiches, and water to feed the men and show appreciation for their efforts. At the command post on Route 8, a Speculator woman supplied lasagna dinners for the entire crew.

The attention was more than welcomed by the stressed officers, whose feelings were well expressed in the comments of Trooper Lawrence Yerdon: "The people up here have been just terrific. They've driven all over the place every day, delivering sandwiches to the men. Nobody asked them to do it. They're doing it because they're good people, and don't think the troopers don't appreciate it."

Outside of the immediate area, the Garrow story was gathering momentum. Already the top news story statewide, it now garnered headlines across the country. Readers in Ohio, Nevada, and California were kept abreast of developments as the chase continued. The drama of the manhunt was a powerful draw, and people everywhere followed the daily reports.

Over the weekend, search leaders received a visit from Onondaga County D.A. Leo Hayes, who praised their efforts. Besides the charges awaiting Garrow in Onondaga County, Hayes revealed the fugitive was now wanted for questioning in several other cases. The city of Syracuse had suffered a spate of unsolved murders and rapes, and Robert Garrow had begun to emerge as a suspect in several of them.

At the top of the victim list was a young girl, Alicia Hauck, who had been missing since July 11. The sixteen-year-old Corcoran High School student failed to return from a summer school class, and Garrow was a person of interest that officials hoped to question on the matter.

Of all the unsolved cases they were saddled with, Syracuse investigators believed Hauck's was the one most likely to have involved Robert Garrow. Capturing him alive was considered crucial if they hoped to solve the Hauck case and several other mysteries.

The hunt continued into the weekend, focusing on the area where officials believed Garrow was hemmed in. Still, being confined to an area of 140 square miles was far from actually being trapped. Garrow had already demonstrated great capability of movement in the woods. Should he manage to cross a highway, it opened a vast new region in which he could roam. Maintaining the search perimeter was critical, but it was a very difficult task.

On Saturday, search officials convened, poring over events of the past week and devising new strategies. One issue they addressed was manpower. Reinforcements were needed to give the men a break from the exhausting, draining ordeal they had endured for seven long days and nights.

To relieve them, a fresh cadre of officers was summoned to man the majority of checkpoints and roadblocks. Key personnel were retained to familiarize the new searchers with what had transpired, and what to expect in the coming days. The veterans of the manhunt were then granted a well-earned respite from a tense situation.

With a pool of about three thousand officers to draw from across the state, search leaders now felt they could maintain pursuit indefinitely. Their number was enhanced by sheriff's deputies, plus a large contingent of conservation officers and forest rangers, the only two groups comfortably working within their milieu.

The decision was made to modify certain search techniques. After locating Garrow's lean-tos, it was felt that troopers had been too methodical, and thus too predictable, in where and how they searched. Teams would now be more mobile, and thus able to employ the element of surprise. Spot searches were conducted in addition to the "game drive" system already in use (a method commonly employed by deer hunters). The combination provided an excellent one-two punch.

The new tactics were intended to help overcome major obstacles in the manhunt. Several of the long-established methods of searching had failed to produce results. Helicopters hadn't been very effective due to the thickness of the ground cover. The use of infrared equipment for night searches had seemed promising, but early in the search, officers discussed the possibility with military representatives. They learned that the dense foliage would render the equipment virtually useless.

Bloodhounds had been effective to a point, but it appeared Garrow was successfully concealing his scent from the dogs. Frequent heavy rain may have helped him in that respect. His greatest advantages were an enormous forest in which to roam, and plenty of camps to raid for supplies. Best of all for Garrow, he was the proverbial needle in a haystack, and this needle didn't want to be found.

On Monday, August 6, with new search guidelines in place,

police were back at the task that had occupied two hundred men for more than a week. They kept plugging away, allowing time for Garrow to make a mistake that might lead to his capture.

It was now day nine of the manhunt, with efforts concentrated on the triangular area a few miles southeast of Speculator, and north of Wells village. Authorities believed they had their quarry somewhat confined there, and that the new measures would help flush him out.

But Robert Garrow had other plans.

3

Through the Dragnet

As search teams executed the new tactics, peripheral support continued at roadblocks on all highways leading to Speculator. For the roadblock teams, most days were a strange combination of tension and drudgery. Methodically searching each vehicle was a tedious process. Conversely, each one held the potential for sudden, deadly danger. Garrow might be secreted within, ready to shoot his way to freedom.

The roadblock crew south of Indian Lake on Route 30, about twenty miles west of Speculator village, briefly escaped the monotony early Monday morning. At 6:20 a.m., a car slowly approached the outpost, and nothing seemed unusual. As it neared the roadblock, officers could see the driver, who appeared to have long hair and didn't seem at all to match the description of Garrow.

The highway obstruction consisted of two police cruisers angled towards the center of the road, blocking most of the highway. Following protocol, the car slowed further. Then, just short of stopping, it suddenly lurched forward, shooting through the gap between the police cars.

Taken by surprise, the men quickly recovered. One officer stayed behind to man the roadblock. The other jumped into a cruiser and took off in pursuit of the vehicle, which enjoyed a considerable head start.

The driver of the car clearly had no intentions of slowing down. As the chase continued, the troop car exceeded one hundred miles per hour and began making gains. Together they hurtled along Route 30 for several miles. Then, in a puff of smoke, it all ended. The police cruiser had closed to within a half mile, but an engine malfunction put the car out of commission. There would be no further pursuit.

Attempts were made to contact other patrol cars and the Saranac Lake substation, but radio transmission was notoriously unreliable in the Adirondacks due to the rough, mountainous terrain. Whoever the violator was, he was long gone. Police surmised the car held some type of contraband that the driver feared would be found during the roadblock search.

Meanwhile, between Speculator and Wells, teams of armed officers resumed the week-old search with renewed vigor. Some performed spot checks, hoping to surprise Garrow and flush him from hiding, while others conducted hunting-style drives through the woods.

At about 3:30 that afternoon, a stolen-vehicle report came in from Deerfoot Lodge, a Christian camp located about five miles northwest of Speculator. Situated on scenic Whitaker Lake deep in the woods off Route 30, the camp was well known in the area.

The likelihood of a connection between Garrow and the missing car seemed doubtful. The camp complex was about seven miles northwest of where he was believed to be hiding, and the intensified search effort along Routes 8 and 30 in all probability had restricted Garrow's movement.

Still, every lead was important until it could be dismissed. Troopers were dispatched to evaluate the report and examine the scene. In the meantime, the search continued as planned. The last ten days must have taken a toll on Garrow, and it was deemed critical to escalate the pressure. If the bugs, the heat, or hunger didn't get to him, the incessant pursuit might wear him down to the point of surrender.

At Deerfoot Lodge, detectives determined that the missing vehicle was a white Pontiac bearing Ohio license plates. Regional law enforcement agencies were immediately notified, and a report came in of a similar vehicle at Inlet, twenty-five miles northwest of Speculator across a vast wilderness, and sixty-five miles distance by highway.

Further investigation revealed it to be an older, disabled car belonging to an owner who lived nearby. It was just another of many false alarms.

A short time later, after speaking with the owner of the

Pontiac, investigators at Deerfoot Lodge contacted headquarters with critical information. Though the crime had been reported at 3:30 p.m., the vehicle had actually disappeared from the parking lot before dawn.

There was immediate alarm. At Indian Lake, it was a white car that had breached the roadblock and escaped about twelve hours earlier.

The search for the missing vehicle was stepped up, and a description of the stolen car was transmitted to all agencies across the region. If Garrow had taken it, he could be out there somewhere among the public, a potentially deadly danger to anyone he might encounter. Notified of the latest developments, Syracuse authorities kept a close eye on Garrow's city home.

Then, late in the evening, stunning news. A woman operating a gas station in North Creek, about twenty-five miles northeast of Speculator, reportedly sold $5 worth of gas to the operator of a white motor vehicle bearing Ohio license plates. Furthermore, she was "95 percent sure" that the man who purchased the gas was none other than Robert Garrow.

The story unfolded at Whispering Pines Mobil Station, owned jointly by Betty Baker and her mother. Betty had observed the car entering the gas pump area from the direction of North Creek. The male driver just sat in his car, waiting for someone to come out, but Betty was short of help and said he would have to pump the gas himself.

The man resisted, displaying a real reluctance to get out of the car. After remaining seated for a minute or two, he finally did so, telling Betty he didn't know how to operate the pump. She offered to instruct him from the doorway, so he came closer to the building and held five dollars out at arm's length to pay for the gas.

Betty Baker recalled later, "I took the money, and he just glared right through me." As she guided him through the process, Baker struck up a conversation, first about the weather, and then about the Garrow manhunt.

When she asked about roadblocks, the stranger mentioned one at the nearby junction of Routes 28N and 28. This aroused suspicion on Betty's part, and when she raised the matter twice more, he stuck to his story. She knew of no such roadblocks near the village.

Treading carefully, Betty wondered aloud what might have happened that required a new roadblock. His answer skirted the issue: "There's been a lot of strange things happening lately." The verbal jousting between them indicated her suspicions, which he sensed. She was broaching a dangerous subject, but the man maintained a friendly demeanor.

By this time, he had stopped the pump just short at $4.99. Betty told him one more squeeze would do it. He tried, but the pump jumped to $5.05. The man apologized repeatedly, and friendly banter ensued between them regarding the extra five cents. All the while, Betty tried to get a look at the car's license plate, but he positioned himself strategically to block it.

She persisted, and finally the man left without receiving his change. Nothing in his behavior had suggested he was anything other than a gentleman. And, if it *was* Robert Garrow, it took tremendous chutzpah for him to chat about the manhunt.

Betty Baker had followed her instincts, engaging in a cat-and-mouse game, unfazed by her opponent. She had suspected his identity all along, and as he drove away, she succeeded in capturing his plate number.

Police were notified, and officers were sent to North Creek to secure the scene. But early on, the consensus was that it could not have been Garrow. Roadblocks stood in dozens of locations, and the armed troopers at each barricade were familiar with the suspect's appearance and description. It seemed highly unlikely he had made it through the widespread network of obstructions.

As a precaution, the homes of Garrow's relatives in Mineville, Witherbee, and Port Henry were placed under surveillance. If he was that far north, he might be planning a visit to his hometown.

Police continued to follow up on the stolen car, but as far as they knew, Garrow was still in the Speculator area, where the search continued. There was not enough definite information to move operations elsewhere and abandon the Lake Pleasant site. Reports of camp burglaries were still coming in, and bloodhounds, helicopters, and foot patrols were still on the case.

With the gas station incident and all the ups and downs of

the past week, the manhunt story was rapidly becoming a public relations nightmare for police. It was about to get much worse.

Tuesday morning brought a shocking revelation. Garrow had paid a late-night visit to the Witherbee home of his sister, Agnes Mandy.

During the brief stop, Agnes called Edith in Syracuse to ask for a pair of glasses for Garrow (he had lost his at the Domblewski scene). The Mandy phone was being monitored, and after the call was intercepted, police paid a visit to the home in the early hours of Tuesday morning. But they were too late. Garrow had once again vanished.

Following interviews with the Mandys, officers redoubled their efforts, finally locating the stolen Pontiac south of Witherbee at the end of Chipmunk Lane, a dirt road leading into dense woods. The car was being examined for fingerprints and other evidence, but the conclusion was obvious.

Newspaper reporters obtained confirmation of the visit from Garrow's sixteen-year-old nephew, David, who said his uncle was unarmed and didn't want anyone to get hurt, but had a "heavy fear of returning to jail." It was unclear how anyone could get hurt if he was unarmed.

So it was true! Garrow had somehow lived up to his phantom persona, eluding hundreds of searchers time and time again. He had managed to avoid capture by the largest manhunt force in the annals of New York State crime fighting.

But how had he done it?

The escape from Speculator required persistence, daring, hubris, and great luck, all in appreciable quantities. In Garrow's case, the supply seemed unlimited.

As new search guidelines were designed and introduced during the past weekend, Garrow had somehow made his way to remote Deerfoot Lodge, several miles west of Speculator village. In the lodge parking lot, he found a white Pontiac with the keys inside, along with some clothing, a wig, and a pair of wire-rimmed glasses. By all measures, his good fortune was already remarkable. But it gets better.

Making full use of the items to disguise his appearance, it was Garrow who had approached the roadblock at Indian

Lake, suddenly gunning the engine to make a successful, wild getaway. Luck struck again when both the fan belt and power steering belt on the pursuit car failed, forcing police to abandon the chase.

His good fortune continued when the mountainous terrain prevented police radio contact with other patrol vehicles, ensuring his successful escape.

At Indian Lake village, Garrow followed Route 30 north through Blue Mountain Lake and Long Lake. About forty miles from Indian Lake, near the south end of Tupper Lake, he pulled off the highway onto a logging road. In the vicinity of Route 421 and Horseshoe Lake, Garrow hid the car in the woods.

Finding an elevated site where he could keep an eye on the vehicle, he spent most of the day sleeping and resting. Finally, as darkness arrived, he took to the road again.

By now, the car was running perilously low on fuel. Considering all his options, Garrow decided to head for familiar territory. Backtracking through the mountains, he passed through Indian Lake, and about eighteen miles farther down the road at North Creek, he stopped for gas and chatted with Betty Baker.

From there, it was only about an hour's drive to Witherbee, where Garrow visited his sister. He arrived during the 11:00 p.m. local news broadcast, and was at his sister's home for no more than ten minutes, time enough for a brief chat and to grab some food. When TV newscasters reported that Garrow was believed to be driving a stolen car, he left the home immediately and went into hiding.

And what of the police detail assigned to monitor the Mandy house? The men had received information about a suspicious vehicle elsewhere in the village and left briefly to check it out. For Garrow, whether deceit was involved or the timing was simply fortuitous, the results were the same. During their short absence, he had already come and gone. Lady Luck, indeed.

From Speculator, Garrow had navigated a seemingly impenetrable network of obstacles and had driven over one hundred miles, untouched. The entire saga strained credulity. When the full story hit the newspapers, a series of emotions spread across northern New York.

Widespread fear had already prompted citizens everywhere to lock their doors, travel in pairs, and buy firearms, or keep the ones they already owned loaded and at the ready. A siege mentality had infiltrated every community from the central Adirondacks to the US–Canada border, seventy miles north of Witherbee.

Now, fear was heightened to the verge of panic, spawned by disbelief. A dangerous killer, hunted by two hundred law officers for nine days and hemmed in by roadblocks, had suddenly surfaced more than sixty miles away. Somehow, he eluded authorities, breached the most comprehensive dragnet in New York State history, and was still on the loose. It was baffling to police, the media, and the public how Garrow could have pulled off such an improbable feat.

And if he *had* done it, then anything was possible. Reports began coming in from all directions, hundreds of miles apart. Garrow was seen in Champlain near the Canadian border, in Glens Falls, in Syracuse, and in any number of communities across the northern part of the state. The story's effect was at once mind-boggling and terrifying.

With confirmation that Garrow had been seen, most of the Speculator search force was immediately dispatched to Witherbee. A perimeter of thirty roadblocks was established surrounding the Mineville area, and posters of Garrow were shown to all citizens at every roadblock in the hopes that someone could offer a solid lead as to his whereabouts.

Bloodhounds and search crews combed the woods around Witherbee and Mineville, but nothing was found. Police were forced to issue the discomfiting report that there was no sign of the fugitive, and that he may have already left the area.

Authorities in neighboring Vermont were contacted with details of the case. Witherbee is only a few miles from Lake Champlain, which separates Vermont and New York State. The ferry system that services the lake was put under continuous police watch, as was the Crown Point Bridge nearby, and the bridge at Rouses Point, far to the north.

Canadian and American customs officials were also alerted,

and police checkpoints were established along the border. Hundreds of miles to the southeast, Garrow's home remained under constant surveillance by Syracuse police. Though he might try to flee north into Canada, officials felt there was a stronger likelihood he would try to reach his family.

Garrow's sister, Florence, was also contacted in Schenectady. Fearing for the safety of her children, she agreed to inform officials if her brother stopped to visit.

More than one hundred police officers were now hunting for Garrow in the Witherbee area, and a house-to-house search was conducted in the vicinity of where the stolen car was found. But interviewing family members, combing the woods, and searching homes all yielded the same results: nothing. There was a very real fear and growing belief that he had already left the area.

Though a small contingent of about thirty men remained at Speculator, all the action was now at Witherbee. Helicopters hovered overhead and search teams with bloodhounds hunted the mountainside. Armed guards occupied the thirteen roadblocks in the immediate vicinity of Witherbee village.

Despite the intensity of the efforts, not a shred of evidence was found. If Garrow was still around, he was managing to stay at least one step ahead of his pursuers.

Attorney Frank Armani took the unorthodox step of issuing a public appeal to his missing client, imploring Garrow to surrender. The plea was kept on a generic level to avoid implying guilt, and for fear of compromising Armani's possible future representation of Garrow in court.

On Wednesday, August 8, Day 11 of the manhunt, New York's most notorious criminal remained at large. Police said the suspect might now be clad in a gray sweatshirt with the words "Michigan State" prominently featured. State Police Major Donald Ambler noted that Garrow's photograph had been posted at more than twenty roadblocks from the Adirondacks all the way to the Canadian border.

A day after the stolen car was found, forensic experts confirmed the presence of Garrow's fingerprints on the vehicle. With that announcement, the number of searchers at the scene was nearly doubled to around two hundred. Police ratcheted up the pressure, repeatedly questioning Agnes Mandy, though she provided little information. Ambler noted that charges of aiding a fugitive were being considered.

One ominous note did surface from interviews with Garrow's family members. He had repeatedly vowed never to return to a prison cell, very threatening words from a man carrying a high-powered rifle. The statement suggested two possibilities: a shootout to the death, or suicide. For several reasons, neither was a desired outcome.

On Thursday, police began their third day of searching the Witherbee area, and the twelfth day overall of the manhunt. Despite roadblocks, bloodhounds, helicopters, and a small army of men on the case, Garrow somehow managed to remain invisible. In light of his successful escape from Speculator, troopers voiced fears that he may have once again slipped away.

Then, a report came in of a burglary on Silver Hill Road. A bloodhound was brought to the scene, detecting a scent trail that led into the woods. It seemed a pretty strong indication that this was the work of Garrow. Who else but a desperate criminal would commit such an act in a tiny village virtually crawling with police?

The decision was made to bring in reinforcements and cordon off the area. Men were assigned to establish a perimeter along Silver Hill Road, waiting and watching for any movement in the woods.

At the same time, unbeknownst to the officers on deployment, another break had occurred nearby at the Mandy home. Garrow's nephew was spied carrying a bag into a wooded area. When police confronted him, they discovered the bag contained food, apparently intended for his fugitive uncle.

After questioning Mandy briefly, police ordered the evacuation of several homes in the vicinity, and a team of troopers entered the wooded area, led by a bloodhound. In quick fashion, the dog picked up a trail and began moving rapidly through the brush.

Meanwhile, the contingent of men lining the perimeter was unaware there was a bloodhound detail at work until the dog was heard barking excitedly. In effect, they were now hunters on watch, waiting while others drove game in their direction. In this case, the goal was to capture the prey alive, but this prey possessed both the will and the ability to kill.

Though it was thrown together quickly, the plan was working to perfection. While they hadn't actually sighted him, Garrow was on the run from the dog team. As he neared the roadway, the men on watch spotted him and tensed for the final confrontation.

Then, Garrow seemed to suddenly realize his predicament: armed men along the road, and a bloodhound in hot pursuit. There was nowhere to go!

Moving parallel to the highway, occasionally in view of the officers, he abruptly reversed course. The surprise move sent Garrow directly towards the advancing patrol team, which was unaware of his movements.

The need arose for a split-second decision. Should the line of armed men wait, hoping to take him alive, while Garrow, armed with a rifle, raced towards unsuspecting officers?

Among the lawmen lining Silver Hill Road was New York State Trooper Ronald Brooks. Next to him, about fifty yards away, was Saratoga County conservation officer Hillary "Guy" Leblanc, armed with a twelve-gauge shotgun. Leblanc spied Garrow and yelled out, "Robert, Robert, drop the gun. Drop the gun, Robert."

Garrow immediately fled. Leblanc made his decision and opened fire. As he shot, Garrow went down, but regained his footing and continued to flee. Leblanc fired again, then twice more. Garrow went down for a second time, but rose again and ran into the woods. And then there was silence.

After a few minutes, Leblanc told Trooper Brooks that Garrow had fallen twice, but he wasn't sure it was the result of being hit, or if he had simply tripped. Brooks took the lead, instructing Leblanc to cover him as he moved forward to assess the results.

Proceeding cautiously, Brooks located Garrow's escape path. There were droplets of blood visible, confirming that he was injured, but the extent was unknown.

The bloodhound crew arrived, joining Brooks. They followed

the trail, which seemed to split into two directions, causing some confusion. It proved to be no accident. Though wounded, Garrow had doubled back on his route in an effort to avoid capture.

Within minutes, Brooks called out, "There he is." He found the fugitive lying on his back, one leg across the loaded rifle, which was cocked and ready to fire. As Brooks approached, he placed his foot firmly across Garrow's firearm. Garrow rolled his head to the left and opened his eyes. Then, he rolled his head back and closed them again.

Within a few minutes, other men arrived, and the injured prisoner was handcuffed where he lay. Arrangements were begun for transportation to the nearest hospital.

Garrow had told family members that, if capture became imminent, he planned to shoot the first person he encountered so others would return fire and kill him. But for the immediate effects of Garrow's injuries, Trooper Brooks may well have been shot dead as he approached.

And, if Leblanc had not fired when he did, a frantic, desperate Garrow was heading directly towards an unsuspecting bloodhound crew. Either way, a catastrophe had been averted.

Finally, they had their man. At approximately 2:05 p.m. on August 9, 1973, the most massive manhunt in New York State history ended. But the story of Robert F. Garrow was far from over.

4

Pre-Trial Shocks

Senior BCI Investigator Henry McCabe arrived on the scene moments after the shooting. He initially thought Garrow was dead. Before verifying life status, McCabe checked him carefully for any additional weapons and found nothing. Garrow's rifle held four rounds of live ammo, one in the carrier and three in the magazine. Amidst the chaos, he never managed to fire a shot. A hunting knife was embedded in the ground nearby.

Leblanc's aim had been true. The four shots resulted in two minor wounds to Garrow's chest, and two more serious hits to his left arm and left foot. The extent of his injuries was yet to be determined. In light of recent events, there would have been little public sympathy had he died right there in the woods.

From the mountainside at Witherbee, Garrow was taken about fifty miles north to Champlain Valley Physicians Hospital (CVPH) in Plattsburgh. Much to the relief of officials in Warren, Hamilton, and Onondaga Counties, the hospital soon pronounced Garrow's condition as good, and his prognosis as guarded.

A decision was forthcoming on surgery to treat the chest wounds, but his injuries did not require placement in the intensive care unit.

In the aftermath, police charged Garrow's sixteen-year-old nephew with one felony count of hindering prosecution for aiding his uncle by supplying him with food. A few days later he was released on $1,000 bail. (Because of his age, and the fact that a relative was involved, Mandy was never prosecuted.)

Search leaders publicly addressed the manhunt's final moments. Contrary to plans, Garrow had been felled by gunfire rather than captured unharmed. Said State Police Major Don Ambler, "It's too bad that Garrow couldn't be taken without injury, but there is no question in my mind that LeBlanc saved the lives of several of my men by firing."

In reference to Garrow's sudden reversal of course, turning towards the approaching bloodhound team, he added, "This guy was at the end of the game. It was his moment of truth. He had a loaded rifle and only a couple of choices. He could have dropped it, or put it in his mouth and pulled the trigger, or opened up and battled it out to the death."

In fact, days earlier, another of Garrow's sisters, Mrs. Florence Brooks of Schenectady, said, "He'll either kill himself, or they'll have to kill him. I remember him saying one time, 'I'll never go behind bars again. It's too tough. The years of loneliness are just too much for you.' "

Garrow's wife was apprised of the shooting, and with family in tow, Edith left Syracuse for Plattsburgh. At her husband's request, she called Frank Armani, who made the long drive and paid his client a visit in the hospital. He was met with a fervent plea to continue as Robert's legal counsel.

Among the considerations in representing Garrow was his ability to pay. With almost no resources, he would likely qualify for a court-appointed attorney. Armani left Plattsburgh and headed for Lake Pleasant, the Hamilton County seat. The judge there could shed some light on several legal issues confronting Armani should he act as Garrow's counsel.

In the meantime, police and other searchers received praise for finally bringing the manhunt to an end. Not surprisingly, a perception of ineptitude had arisen when Garrow somehow escaped the police dragnet in the Speculator area.

Still, it was the overall intent of search leaders to outlast Garrow while making every effort to capture or contain him. The plan all along was to bring him in alive. Now he was in custody, and from many venues, officials were lauded for their persistence in the face of such a daunting, dangerous task.

Investigators were anxious to question Garrow on several topics, particularly the whereabouts of Susan Petz. The murders of Domblewski and Porter were also high on the priority list, but nothing could be done to help those two victims.

Petz, however, might still be held captive somewhere,

invoking a sense of urgency in determining her whereabouts. All efforts were focused on finding the missing girl, and police believed Garrow held the key to solving that mystery.

Syracuse police were also eager to interrogate Garrow, the prime suspect in several open cases. Two officers were sent to Plattsburgh within twenty-four hours of his capture to question him on numerous unsolved crimes, and about two teenage girls who were still missing. The stories of Karen Levy and Alicia Hauck had been featured prominently in the Syracuse media, and it was suspected that Garrow held the answers to both.

In his fifth-floor room at CVPH in Plattsburgh, the hospital's newest patient chatted freely with family, including Edith and Robert, Jr. They talked about many things, but spoke nothing of the crimes Garrow was suspected of committing.

With others, he was much less obliging. Henry McCabe of the BCI was thwarted in repeated attempts to get any useful information from Garrow. While lying in his hospital bed, Robert was questioned about the Domblewski and Petz cases, but revealed nothing.

He claimed to be in too much pain for lengthy interviews, but Barbara Seguin, a hospital supervisor, noted of her newest patient, "He's very, very nice with the staff and extremely polite. But around police, he's quite stubborn and closemouthed."

With no information forthcoming from Garrow, the search for Petz continued, but prospects were bleak. She had been missing now for nearly four weeks, and police had no solid leads. They only had Garrow, and he wasn't talking.

Mrs. Earl Petz, Susan's mother, spoke candidly with reporters about her daughter, saying, "It's pretty obvious she is dead." Mrs. Petz had good reason to be talking with members of the written media, explaining that Susan's career goal was to become a newspaper reporter. While a student at Boston University, she had worked as many as forty hours per week on a community newspaper.

With sad irony, Mrs. Petz noted that Susan was supposed to be obtaining her degree that very week. Now she was gone, and it appeared she might never be found.

A week after Garrow's capture, he was still in the hospital

and still wasn't talking. With no new information to report, the local media relegated the once-sensational story to the background. While that was true in the Adirondacks, Garrow's name was still headline fodder statewide.

The fight was intensifying between D.A. Leo Hayes and the state parole board over Garrow's records. An effort was under way to place the blame for Garrow's crimes on the heads of certain officials. As often happens, a high-profile criminal case was becoming a political issue, with careers on the line.

The subpoena by Hayes ordered Joseph Maxwell, area parole supervisor, to produce minutes of Garrow's June parole hearing, along with "all records relating to the conduct of Robert F. Garrow since he was placed on parole on or about the 12th day of August, 1968."

The parole board, a division of the Department of Correctional Services, said the records could not be surrendered except for details of an inmate's criminal background. Despite that claim, Hayes felt he had a strong argument. Garrow's rap sheet seemed to indicate he should have been held in custody until the new sex charges had been investigated.

However, neither Geddes police nor the district attorney's office had been notified that the judge was even considering Garrow's release on bail.

Further enraging Hayes was that, despite the serious charges Garrow faced in the abduction of the two young girls, a parole-hearing officer had concluded that "probable cause for a revocation did not exist."

Again, just as they weren't notified of the bail hearing, area law-enforcement officials were not informed of the decision allowing Garrow to remain free on parole. Neither the judge nor the parole officer recognized the need to keep him off the streets. His release had since proven disastrous.

Perhaps protecting its own interests, the state now refused to release Garrow's parole record, claiming it was privileged information. The issue became one for the courts to decide.

As the arguments between Hayes and the parole board made headlines, the public began to realize what officials already knew: a convicted felon rapist had been arrested on charges of serious sex crimes; the accused had been released to await trial more than a month later; and, in the interim, he had likely murdered several people, and possibly committed several rapes.

Newspapers across the state, and especially in the Syracuse area, were flooded with letters and editorials criticizing this unthinkable sequence of events. Anger was the common denominator. The safety net created to protect the public had failed miserably. For many citizens, life would never be the same, and they expressed their outrage.

As for the Adirondacks, no longer could visitors feel safe while camping, hiking, swimming, or even picnicking. The Garrow story had changed all that. The combined effects of lax court rulings, vicious crimes, unlikely escapes, and the lengthy manhunt left a dark cloud over every outing. There was no feeling of security left, especially in the mountains. For a generation of hikers, the innocence was gone, permanently.

In Hamilton County, District Attorney Intemann announced that a grand jury would convene to consider charges against Garrow in the Domblewski murder. Onondaga County authorities also sought him on the charges listed in Judge Ormand Gale's bench warrant of July 27, and he was still a suspect in many other crimes.

As the grand jury met, another major development occurred. North of Syracuse, near Sylvan Beach, a body was found floating in Black Creek. The corpse was nude, and so badly decomposed that determination of even the simplest factors of sex, age, and race would require an autopsy.

Two of the missing girls from Syracuse, Martha Allen and Karen Levy, were mentioned as possibilities. However, preliminary indications were that the body was approximately 5 feet 4 inches tall, three inches taller than Levy. Allen was a much closer match. The next name to surface was Susan Petz.

Major difficulties were encountered in analyzing the recovered body. DNA profiling was fifteen years away, and the primary means of victim identification was dental records. But this corpse was found to have excellent teeth, leaving nothing to pursue in that area.

Several days later, despite extensive testing by a team

of professionals, only a few basics had been ascertained. The deceased was female, about 5 feet 3 inches tall, and perhaps 125 pounds. It had taken the combined efforts of the county coroner, an x-ray technician, an orthodontist, and a pathologist to arrive at that minimal description.

The name of Petz was finally eliminated from consideration when it was verified that Susan did, in fact, have dental records. Of course, there remained the distinct possibility the woman was one of Garrow's many other suspected victims.

On the legal front, after meeting with Hamilton County Judge George W. Marthen in Lake Pleasant, Frank Armani had agreed to serve as Garrow's court-appointed representative. Armani had never handled a murder case, and to help with the actual trial activities, he successfully petitioned lawyer Francis Belge to join him in Garrow's defense. In a very unusual move, the judge agreed in principle to the use of two court-appointed attorneys, but reserved judgment on the final ruling.

Unlike Frank Armani, Francis Belge possessed an outgoing personality. He was popular with women, and as much at home in a barroom as a courtroom. Well known in the Syracuse region, Belge was a skilled trial lawyer and the perfect complement to Armani's diligent research efforts and technical capabilities. Working as a team, they prepared to defend Garrow against the serious charges facing him.

As D.A. Intemann announced earlier, the grand jury had been reconvened to study the Garrow case. Carol Malinowski, David Freeman, and Nicholas Fiorillo testified, and each identified their attacker as Garrow.

On August 21, 1973, the grand jury returned eight sealed indictments. It was obvious to all that Garrow's murder charge was among the eight, but Judge Marthen confirmed the indictments would remain sealed until the accused had been officially arraigned.

Since there was no easy path to defending Robert Garrow, Belge opted for aggressive tactics, feeling it was best to strike early and hard. In response to the announcement of sealed indictments, the defense team called a press conference. Their intent was to address the prosecution's mishandling of the case thus far.

One day prior to the press conference, Belge fired the first salvo, saying, "I believe that maybe some prosecutors should be reminded, in bold print, what the canon of ethics is all about."

Those words would eventually come back to haunt him, and add great irony to his role in the Garrow case.

The statement had the intended effect, stoking the ire of his opponents. The actual press conference promised even more fireworks, and Francis Belge didn't disappoint. Garrow's case had already gained headlines across the country. Savoring the attention, Belge entered the fray with elbows flying. Armani's nickname for his colorful partner was "Balls," and it was easy to see why.

By his reckoning, the release of Garrow's records, plus comments to the media by prosecutors, made it impossible for his client to receive a fair trial. Belge further accused the prosecution of trying their case in public instead of allowing due process to run its course.

Of the attorneys Belge was referring to, the main target was Leo Hayes, who had stirred up a huge public debate with his attempt to obtain Garrow's parole records. The defense countered that releasing Garrow's record to the media was a "clear violation" of the American Bar Association's Canon of Ethics governing pre-trial publicity.

To support that assertion, Belge took a stance that endeared him to reporters but thoroughly rankled Hayes. The culprit, he said, was not the media for publishing the information, but rather the D.A.'s office for revealing it. In effect, the defense was playing by the rules, while the prosecution had breached legal boundaries in order to bolster their case.

With that, the battle over Garrow's parole records heated up considerably. Hayes wanted them made available, but the state attorney general's office adamantly refused.

At the same time, a legal precedent for such situations was playing out on the national stage in the Watergate scandal. Both parties in the Garrow case turned their attention to events that transfixed the nation, as President Richard Nixon refused to hand over tapes that he considered privileged information.

On August 29, 1973, Judge John Sirica of the U.S. District Court issued a subpoena ordering Nixon to turn over certain recordings, a decision that would be appealed with great vigor. Similar issues were at stake in the faceoff over Garrow's records, which had been subpoenaed by Hayes.

Both sides knew that the outcome of the federal case would impact their own battle, and New York's high court would make no determination until the Nixon case was settled. For the time being, the parole issue was sidelined.

In Syracuse, William Hauck, father of missing teenager Alicia Hauck, spoke to reporters on September 11, the two-month anniversary of his daughter's disappearance. Hauck expressed hope they would find her, but authorities still had no evidence and no leads.

Bloodhounds and aircraft had been used in the ongoing search, and Alicia's name and photograph were featured prominently in Syracuse newspapers. A $1,000 reward was offered for any solid information, but no one came forward. All along, the suspicions of detectives rested on Robert Garrow, but he remained silent.

In mid-September, Dr. Donald Kasprzak of CVPH in Plattsburgh announced that his patient was doing extremely well and was nearly ready to be released. Police made plans to transfer Garrow from the hospital to the Hamilton County Jail.

Four shotgun pellets were still embedded in Garrow, and they would not be removed. The wounds were allowed to heal, but the prisoner remained in a wheelchair, apparently unable to walk despite doctors' assessments of his injuries as superficial. In fact, Kasprzak's official report indicated there was "no restriction of the movement of Robert F. Garrow's left leg."

On September 19, 1973, forty-one days after being gunned down in Witherbee, Garrow was returned to the custody of New York State police. Major Donald Ambler assigned six armed troopers to accompany the prisoner on the three-hour drive to Lake Pleasant.

For much of his hospitalization, Garrow had been featured only occasionally in the media, but suddenly his name was everywhere. Headlines and bylines featured "the balding, thirty-seven-year-old bakery mechanic," the "bespectacled killer," or the "convicted rapist." Stories of his past crimes and suspected offenses were reiterated on radio, television, and in newspapers.

Garrow's indictment remained sealed until his arrival at Lake Pleasant in Hamilton County, three miles south of Speculator. After a brief stop at the jail, he was moved next door to the courthouse, where a series of thirteen counts was read by Judge Marthen. The most serious among the charges was the murder of Philip Domblewski.

Garrow, chained to his wheelchair, pleaded innocent to all charges and was ordered confined to the Hamilton County Jail. Sheriff Arthur Parker had anticipated security requirements for the lockup's newest resident, doubling the guard force to ensure he was monitored at all times. While Garrow was incarcerated, his lawyers began the long, difficult job of preparing his defense.

Onondaga County prosecutors were just as interested in Garrow as were their Hamilton County counterparts. In mid-October, Judge Ormand Gale signed an order temporarily releasing Garrow to the custody of the Onondaga County Sheriff's Department.

The state's best-known prisoner was brought to Syracuse on charges relating to the abduction and sexual assault of the two young girls from Geddes. During a brief court session, eleven charges were read to Garrow. He pleaded innocent to all of them.

His next court appearance was scheduled for the following Tuesday back in Hamilton County. Judge Gale granted Armani's request to detain Garrow for the weekend in the Public Safety Building at Syracuse, allowing the attorneys time to meet with their client and prepare his defense.

In late October, both Armani and Belge appeared in Lake Pleasant before Judge Marthen on behalf of Garrow, who remained in his jail cell next door. The attorneys filed a motion seeking a court-ordered psychiatric evaluation of their client.

At the same hearing, the judge received an appeal from Garrow for court-appointed legal representation on the grounds of indigency. He further requested that Armani and Belge be assigned as his public defenders. Marthen accepted the request for psychiatric testing, but reserved judgment on Garrow's application for multiple public defenders.

Elsewhere, one of the legal issues that could affect Garrow's court case came to a resolution of sorts. In mid-November, the Onondaga County district attorney's office announced it was abandoning the quest for Garrow's parole records.

The official reason given was that "the interests of orderly prosecution outweigh the matter of Garrow's parole records." The office wished in no way to delay or hinder the prosecution of one of New York State's most notorious criminals.

A week later, Robert Garrow's name once again made headlines across the state. In what some termed a shocking development, Garrow was found unconscious in his cell, with a puncture wound to his right arm.

Armani termed the incident a suicide attempt. If he was correct, it would probably have been classified as feeble, at best. The attending physician said Garrow had fallen asleep after the effort, and the superficial injury had clotted on its own.

D.A. Intemann said the wound was self-inflicted, but stopped short of calling it a suicide try. BCI Investigator Richard Beckwith agreed, citing minor damage that required only cursory attention from a doctor.

The self-clotting wound certainly cast doubt on the suicide theory. With his exceptional physical strength, Garrow would have been expected to inflict far more damaging results. Perhaps it was meant to lay the groundwork for proving his insanity or mental instability.

It also may have been a failed escape effort, feigning serious injury to lure a lone deputy into the cell. Garrow had confided to his lawyers that he was devising an escape plan. To discourage him, they cautioned that snipers awaited any such attempt.

By the end of November, most of the psychiatric testing requested by Garrow's attorneys was completed. Based on the doctors' findings, arguments would soon be presented to the court in a competency hearing.

A ruling of incompetency would relegate Garrow to the confines of a mental institution, with the possibility his case might never go to trial. Should he be found competent, it could take several months to prepare a defense. Either way, it seemed certain the Garrow name would disappear from the media for an extended period.

But the case took a sudden, gruesome twist, and just two days after completion of the psychiatric tests, Robert Garrow was back in the headlines.

On Saturday morning, December 1, two children playing in the woods near Witherbee made a horrifying discovery. In an abandoned mine airshaft they spied a human foot in a sneaker, and ran to tell their parents. Police were notified, and with the help of mining engineers, a body was recovered in the early afternoon.

Using dental charts, positive identification was made. Less than a mile from where Robert Garrow had collapsed in a barrage of gunfire, the body of Susan Petz had finally been found. It was barely a half mile from the home of Garrow's parents, where he spent much of his childhood.

No official cause of death was given, but police said there was an apparent stab wound to the heart. It did indeed sound like the murderous handiwork of Robert Garrow.

This was a compelling development, covered by all the major media. Here were the makings of a bona fide serial killer. It now appeared that Garrow had three victims, all strangers to him, and all killed with a knife.

Nothing had been proven yet, of course, and there were no official links established between the deaths. But speculation centered on the obvious conclusion: Garrow had killed Porter, Petz, and Domblewski. Nobody knew how many others he might have slain.

For many officials and for members of her family, Susan's death had been a foregone conclusion, but the grisly discovery of her remains brought reality home. She was gone forever, and at the hands of a monster the likes of which the Adirondack Mountains had never seen.

While the family dealt with the terrible news, prosecutors resolved that Susan had not died in vain. Until then, there had been no charges in the case because there had been no victim. The discovery of her body provided crucial evidence, and it was now up to investigators to connect the dots.

Susan's remains were taken to a Port Henry funeral parlor and prepared for shipment home to her family in Skokie, Illinois. Few details were released by police, except that she died from a single stab wound to the left side of the chest. Since there was no blood or other evidence at the immediate scene, authorities believed it was unlikely she was killed where she was found.

Plans were made to question Garrow further now that Petz's body had been recovered. When the media asked Armani about the possibility, he said, "I see no connection between this and Garrow. Why should they question just him?" As of late Sunday, the day after the body was found, no one had contacted Armani about speaking to his client.

Suggestions of Garrow's link to Petz's death played across the media all week long, but the prisoner refused to talk. Laboratory personnel and investigators worked hard to find an evidentiary link. Garrow's clothing and personal effects, plus items found in his own car and the car he had stolen, were still being examined.

It was painstaking, tedious work comparing hairs, fibers, and other elements. The science of forensics was a valuable tool in the 1970s, but drastically limited in comparison to DNA typing and other methods that were developed decades after Garrow's crimes were committed.

Just as media coverage of the Petz discovery began to subside, Syracuse newspapers exploded with headlines about another possible Garrow victim. On December 8, a week after Susan Petz's body was found in Witherbee, the decomposed remains of sixteen-year-old Alicia Hauck were found in Oakwood Cemetery in Syracuse. She had been missing for five months.

Dozens of officials from various agencies responded to the scene, including Syracuse police, the Onondaga County district attorney's office, the medical examiner's office, and Syracuse University security police. Oakwood Cemetery abutted the grounds of Syracuse University. It was also across the road from Berwyn Avenue, the home of one Robert Garrow.

In the cemetery, a gruesome scene greeted investigators. The body was badly deteriorated, with an arm and the skull separated from the skeleton. Such decomposition likely resulted from the passage of time, exposure to the elements, and attention from animals. Clothing on the body included only a pair of jeans, and nothing above the waist. A ring was recovered, and nearby lay a history textbook and a pair of shoes.

Discovered by a Syracuse University student, the body was in a brushy, wooded, unused portion of the cemetery. Investigators scoured the grounds for hours, looking for any clue that might develop into a solid lead. Considering the situation, prospects were not good.

The confirmation of Hauck's death was a blow to the city of Syracuse. Citizens had followed closely the story of her disappearance and the ongoing search. A sophomore at Corcoran High School, Alicia was a graduate of Our Lady of Lourdes grammar school. She was a cheerleader for the Catholic Youth Organization (CYO) basketball team, as well as the team for Corcoran High. She also belonged to the Humane Society of Central New York, and was a member of a junior bowling league. Her father, William Hauck, was the owner and manager of a bowling center.

The story had become familiar to city residents, and for months, hope was maintained that she would be found alive. Now, the worst fears of all had been realized, as Alicia likely suffered a brutal end. The daughter, the cheerleader, the bowler, the animal-lover, and the student—all were gone. And all eyes turned to Robert Garrow.

Attorneys Armani and Belge had nothing further to say about the Petz or Hauck discoveries, and neither did their infamous client. The lawyers were preparing for trial while awaiting results of the various psychiatric tests Garrow had undergone. It was still possible he would be found unfit to face the court system.

In late December, additional psychological testing on Garrow was completed in Utica. Final assessments were expected within a week, but it soon became apparent that investigators hadn't been sitting idle while awaiting test results.

Authorities announced in early January 1974 that representatives from Essex, Hamilton, Onondaga, and Warren counties would meet to review and share the details from a series of crimes. It was anticipated that a trade of information might reveal links pointing towards a single perpetrator.

The chief cases of concern all involved victims of murder: Susan Petz, discovered in Witherbee in Essex County; Petz's companion, Daniel Porter, found dead in Warren County; Alicia Hauck, recovered from a Syracuse cemetery in Onondaga County; and Philip Domblewski, slain in Hamilton County. In at least some of the investigators' minds, the common denominator was Robert Garrow.

The main suspect in this string of horrors was facing still more testing. Psychiatric examinations thus far addressed his ability to stand trial for the murder of Domblewski in Hamilton County. However, those findings would not be applicable to charges filed in Onondaga County. Accordingly, Garrow was scheduled for another series of tests to be administered at State University Hospital in Syracuse.

At the same time, a bit of good news arrived for the defense team, though it actually mattered little in the overall scheme of things. The federal felony charge filed during the manhunt had been dropped. The violation was in connection to Garrow's purchase of a rifle while concealing an earlier felony conviction.

Penalties under the Federal Firearms Act included a maximum of five years in prison and a $5,000 fine. The government announced they were dropping the charge in consideration of "the weight of the state charges against him."

For psychiatric testing in Onondaga County, Garrow was transferred to the Public Safety Building in Syracuse. The sessions began in mid-January, and were expected to last until the end of the month. Onondaga County lawmen were anxious to question Garrow in the death of Alicia Hauck, but Armani forbade any contact between lawmen and his client. The sole purpose of his presence in Syracuse was completion of the requisite mental examinations.

The work conducted by psychiatrists and psychologists in such cases can serve a variety of purposes. If testing is ordered by the court to determine competency to stand trial, there are two critical issues to address: a defendant's ability to understand the charges, and the capability of a defendant to assist in his or her own defense.

Other types of psychiatric testing often come into play, primarily in murder cases, and especially when a plea of insanity is involved. In 1974, to be declared insane in court matters, the law stated:

> A person is not responsible for criminal conduct if at the time of such conduct, as a result of mental disease or defect, a person lacks substantial capacity either to appreciate the wrongfulness of his conduct or to conform his conduct to the requirements of the law.

Simply put, perpetrators bore no guilt if mental issues clouded their ability to discern right from wrong, or to behave properly. That law conferred great legal weight upon the opinions and conclusions of professionals chosen to conduct mental evaluations. Doctors were often as important as attorneys in murder cases, which might never reach trial if incompetency was the final determination.

On February 8, 1974, based on the results of court-ordered testing requested by the defense, Judge Marthen found Robert Garrow mentally and physically competent to stand trial on charges related to the murder of Philip Domblewski.

Less than two weeks after Marthen's ruling on Garrow's competency, psychiatric testing assumed added importance in the case. Armani announced that his client would plead insanity. At the next court appearance set for February 22, he planned to question the psychiatrist to determine which tests had convinced him that Garrow was competent to stand trial.

Armani pointed out that the state's burden of proof was now two-fold: they would have to prove that Garrow was guilty of murder, and also that he was legally sane.

However, since details of the extensive testing had not yet been revealed, the onus could well fall on Armani and Belge to instead prove Garrow's insanity. Such a plea indicated he had committed the crime he was charged with, but was mentally impaired at the time. Depending on test results, that might be a difficult case to prove.

Armani was doing all he could to buy time. In February, he filed papers with the court, claiming that his client was unable to stand trial due to physical problems that required surgery. Garrow was said to be suffering the lingering effects of injuries sustained during his capture.

Intemann was quick to respond. In an affidavit filed with the court, he offered an in-depth assessment of Garrow's condition based on the findings of two physicians, Dr. Donald Kasprzak and Dr. Frank A. Dick.

Kasprzak was the Plattsburgh doctor who treated Garrow's gunshot wounds, most of which were determined to be superficial. He cited possible damage to the left Achilles tendon as the most serious injury. In the report issued upon Garrow's release from CVPH, Kasprzak said there were no restrictions on the movement of the prisoner's left leg.

Dr. Dick, a resident of Speculator, had tended to Garrow's health since his arrival at the Hamilton County Jail. Dick declared that any type of surgery on Garrow "would serve no useful purpose." He offered specific dates when he had examined and x-rayed Garrow, stating that "the defendant is no longer suffering from the four gunshot wounds received when he was captured, as said wounds are completely healed."

Regarding the arm injury, Dick flatly declared, "the left arm may be used and exercised without discomfort." After again certifying that Garrow's ankle injury had completely healed, Dick addressed the defendant's claim of ongoing back pain, saying it was "entirely subjective, because there is no apparent cause for this problem, as the gunshot wound received in the back was entirely superficial."

In other words, Garrow was faking his disabilities. Those assessments by Doctors Kasprzak and Dick would one day play a role in reshaping the New York State corrections system. For now, it was simply their word against Garrow's, and Garrow claimed he was disabled.

The situation was particularly galling to officers assigned the task of transporting him to court each day. Handicap access ramps were a thing of the future. The men were forced to lift Garrow and his wheelchair from the jail doorway into the courthouse entrance, in spite of the general belief the defendant was as healthy as any of them.

Two additional days of hearings were held as Judge Marthen entertained assorted arguments regarding competency. The defense also requested the grand jury minutes from the session responsible for Garrow's indictment on murder charges.

On March 5, after the hearings ended, Marthen reaffirmed his earlier findings. Robert Garrow was competent to stand trial on the charges laid out in the indictment. There was no further recourse for the defense team. It was time to prepare for trial.

Armani and Belge knew they would need additional psychiatric testing to bolster Garrow's insanity plea. Likewise, the prosecution needed test results to refute his alleged insanity. Until their completion, the examinations sought by both parties would postpone trial proceedings.

With preparations underway, it was apparent that prosecutors had a strong case. The three campers who survived the encounter on the morning of July 29 were prepared to testify, and two of them had listened as Domblewski was slowly murdered. Other witnesses saw Garrow escape the scene, and he was the subject of a highly publicized, twelve-day manhunt.

The preponderance of evidence clearly favored the prosecution, while the defense faced the unenviable task of convincing a jury that Garrow was insane, despite the fact that he had already been found competent to face trial. The two were separate issues, but the jury might well infer a connection.

The defense team did enjoy one advantage: experience. Frank Armani was a successful attorney who aggressively pursued his clients' interests. Francis Belge enjoyed a reputation as one of the top trial lawyers in central New York. With Belge on your side, there was always a chance of winning.

William Intemann, Jr., Hamilton County district attorney, was at the far end of the spectrum from Belge. The position held by Intemann was only part-time, and Hamilton County hadn't hosted a murder trial in forty-five years. The prosecution's resources appeared limited, to say the least.

Still, Intemann was a capable attorney, and he wasn't working alone. During the manhunt for Garrow in the summer of 1973, Onondaga County officials were frequently in touch with search leaders due to pending criminal charges in Syracuse. Among the items discussed was eventual prosecution if Garrow was captured alive.

From those meetings, an agreement arose between Intemann and Jon Holcombe, Onondaga County's chief assistant district attorney, and a man well versed in homicide trials.

Holcombe promised to provide one of his assistants to help with the prosecution of Garrow on murder charges. Besides being a valuable aid to Intemann, Holcombe's representative would provide an inside look at the trial in preparation for future prosecution of Garrow in Onondaga County. It was clearly a mutually beneficial arrangement that would help offset the edge in experience enjoyed by Armani and Belge.

The man chosen by Holcombe to work with Intemann was Assistant D.A. Norman Mordue, a thirty-year-old Vietnam veteran, family man, and graduate of Syracuse University. Though Mordue had not yet prosecuted any murder cases, he had taken part in several homicide investigations.

Holcombe called Mordue "an experienced prosecutor who, in recent months, has specialized in handling cases involving sexual assault charges." Mordue had already been named as lead prosecutor in the pending Onondaga County case against Garrow, and the Hamilton County trial offered excellent preparation for that duty.

In Lake Pleasant court proceedings, Intemann would serve as trial attorney, with Mordue assisting him every step of the way, including strategy and preparation.

The Hamilton County trial of Garrow was set to begin on May 8, but there was another possibility of delay. Armani and Belge petitioned the court for a change of venue in light of the intense negative publicity the twelve-day manhunt had generated. The claim was also made that Hamilton County's miniscule population of 4,700 would render it impossible to select a jury that was not already biased.

Intemann argued there was no evidence from the defense supporting the conclusion that a fair trial could not be obtained. Both attorney teams requested a speedy ruling.

On April 25, the appellate division of the New York State Supreme Court unanimously rejected the request for a change of venue, ordering Garrow to stand trial for murder in Hamilton County court.

With that, the team of Armani and Belge was out of tricks. They now had two weeks to complete final preparations for the defense of their client, the first person to stand trial for murder in Hamilton County since 1929.

5

The Prosecution's Case

Jury duty notices were sent out to three hundred Hamilton County residents. Because the law provided for a minimum of twelve jurors and one alternate, three hundred possibilities seemed more than adequate. The small courtroom could not accommodate anywhere near that many people. Accordingly, seventy-five potential jurors were instructed to report on the first day of selection.

At about 1:30 p.m. on May 8, 1974, Robert Garrow, seated in his wheelchair, was carried up the steps of the Hamilton County courthouse in Lake Pleasant, New York.

At the entrance to the courtroom was a metal detector to scan for weapons and any other contraband. Wooden benches provided seating for fifty spectators. Reporters and jury candidates filled the seats, while many other potential jurors stood to the rear. The defendant was wheeled in and positioned at a table in the center of the courtroom.

Garrow exhibited the same demeanor as he had at most other court appearances. Though his injuries had been pronounced healed by two physicians, he remained wheelchair-bound, his left arm tucked away within his shirt, and his right foot shoeless. And, as had become his habit, Garrow's right hand was frequently used to at least partially mask his face from view.

He was not bound by restraints during court appearances. Judge Marthen had granted a defense request that the defendant not be handcuffed, and that he remain unshackled during transport between the courthouse and the jail next door. The judge assumed Garrow's injuries had left him incapacitated, precluding any risk of escape.

From the pool of three hundred citizens summoned for duty,

the attorneys' job was to trim the group down to potential jurors. When that phase was completed, in-depth questioning would take place to determine who the final jury members would be.

Just prior to starting the selection process, Marthen informed all present that anyone chosen during the first stage would be sequestered for the length of the trial. They were also told not to discuss the case, and to avoid all types of media coverage.

In New York State in the 1970s, people were excused from jury duty on many grounds that have since been eliminated. On the first day, fifty of sixty-five prospects were discharged, mainly for personal reasons that included health problems, the care of dependent family members, and job requirements.

In Hamilton County, employment was largely dependent upon the tourism industry, which was at its height during the summer months. The bulk of many yearly incomes was earned from June through August, and residents had already been hurt financially during the previous year by the lengthy Garrow manhunt. The court was appropriately sympathetic to their circumstances.

On day two, four sheriff's deputies repeated the tedious daily chore of lifting Garrow in his wheelchair and carrying him up the steps of the courthouse. Though the 1970s saw many reforms aiding people with disabilities, it would be years before wheelchair access and handicapped parking spaces became commonplace. The four-man hoist was the solution to getting Garrow into and out of the courtroom.

The second day of jury selection lasted only an hour, raising the pool of potential jurists to twenty-eight. Judge Marthen had indicated he would not allow prospective jurors to be questioned until at least fifty were available. So far, more than one hundred had been excused, including two who admitted they were already prejudiced and could not make a fair judgment. Seventy-five more were scheduled to be in court for the next day's session.

On day three it became clear that selecting potential jurors would take much longer than anticipated. Marthen needed twelve, but he also wanted four alternates, exercising his discretionary power to go beyond the single alternate juror required by law.

By the end of Friday's proceedings, the pool had only reached thirty-three, while more than 150 people had been excused. With the judge's goal set at fifty or more, they were barely halfway there. The process was now expected to last until the end of the following week.

George W. Marthen was well suited to the task at hand. He was a Hamilton County transplant, but had been raised in similar rural surroundings in Wisconsin, spending much of his time hunting and fishing. He attended the New York University School of Law, and, following graduation, spent ten years perfecting his attorney skills in Nassau County, New York.

After moving north to Hamilton County, Marthen was appointed a county judge in 1971, and was then elected to the same position, unopposed, in November of that year. He wore many justice hats in the sparsely populated county, covering family and surrogate court cases with equal ability, and was not at all intimidated by handling a murder trial.

The juror screening process continued into a second week, and as the number of excused citizens mounted, Marthen ordered the sheriff to search voter registration lists for more names. By the end of Wednesday's session, sixty-one potential jurors had been selected, while more than five hundred had been let go.

The court was scheduled to be idle on Saturday and Monday due to prior commitments of the attorneys. Marthen instructed Sheriff Arthur Parker to intensify the hunt for jurists during the break. His plan was to screen two hundred people per day during the coming week.

Never missing a trick, Francis Belge used an unusual tactic during jury selection, hiring a deaf friend who was an expert lip-reader. Recalled Armani many years later, "The D.A. knew people up there, and we didn't. But we only used the woman to read lips during jury selection. She sat with the spectators, and she would tell us when the D.A. whispered something to his assistant that he knew one of them. It was a big help."

As the task of jury selection became more difficult, Marthen raised his goal to at least 150 pool members before beginning the *voir dire* phase of the trial, when the twelve jurors and four alternates would be selected.

However, the judge soon realized the new target was overly ambitious, and almost certain to add another week to the proceedings. By the end of Friday, May 24, the pool of potential jurors numbered 119. Marthen called a recess, declaring that selection of the twelve jurors would begin on the following Wednesday.

More than a thousand people had been screened for service. Many were excused because they were acquainted with members of a witness list that included sixty names. In a region where almost everyone knew everyone else, that criterion presented an obstacle difficult to overcome.

With the screening process as a guide, it appeared the actual jury selection might go on for some time. By Friday, after three days of questioning, ten jurors had been seated. In an effort to finish by week's end, Marthen called a Saturday session.

But, from the thirty pool members screened, only one was chosen. Jury selection would extend into the month of June.

The process certainly seemed snake-bitten. The following week, one juror already chosen was excused due to the death of her husband over the weekend. On Tuesday morning, the twelfth juror was finally selected, much to the relief of everyone.

But on Wednesday, the search for four alternates was still ongoing, and the pool was empty. Sheriff Parker was instructed to bring in more candidates, again delaying the beginning of trial testimony.

Incredibly, the search for alternate juror number four finally met with success during another special Saturday session. After examining more than two thousand potential candidates, approximately 43 percent of the entire Hamilton County population, a jury was now in place. The selection process had lasted exactly one month and one day.

The testimony phase of the trial opened on Monday, June 10, with the defense team offering an insanity plea on Garrow's behalf. On that note, the battle began.

Since Garrow had been uncooperative with doctors performing examinations for the prosecution, William Intemann urged the court to refuse the plea and deny the admission of psychiatric testimony. During testing, the defendant claimed to have no recollection of the Domblewski incident, but had recounted details of the killing for defense psychiatrists. Marthen reserved judgment on the request, and the trial proceeded.

There was solid reasoning behind the state's opposition to an insanity plea. If Garrow's lawyers were successful, their client would be committed to a state mental institution for a specified period. With an eventual finding of permanent incompetency, he might never face the consequences of his crimes.

After opening statements were presented, the prosecution led with two powerful witnesses, Nicholas Fiorillo and Carol Ann (Malinowski) Freeman. Both were camping companions of Domblewski on the morning he was killed, and both had harrowing tales to tell.

Fiorillo described the entire sequence of events that had transpired on the morning of July 29, 1973. He was best friends with Domblewski, and it was the two of them who had risen early to go for breakfast in Wells and do some fishing.

In gripping testimony, he told of the abduction by Garrow, the walk through the woods, and the binding of each other to trees. He described the sounds emitted by Phil during the stabbing, and how Nick had worked vigorously to remove his own restraints, doing so as Domblewski breathed his last.

At the time, Garrow's intense focus on his victim's final moments had allowed Fiorillo to escape. Nick related how he drove to the restaurant in Wells, where the Vodrons helped him contact New York State police in Fonda. Then, he told of leading investigators to the body of his best friend, slumped over and lifeless at the base of a tree.

Carol Malinowski was now Carol Freeman, having married David Freeman in December 1973. Following Fiorillo's testimony, Carol offered her version of what had happened, providing other details of the story. She recalled the first few minutes of the encounter with Garrow at the entrance to the tent, and then all the events leading up to the killing of Domblewski.

As Fiorillo did, Carol recounted listening to Phil's execution, and how she, too, soon managed to remove her bonds. Finding Domblewski soaked in blood and likely dead, she told of scrambling through the forest to the highway, hitching a ride to Speculator, and summoning authorities.

Carol's story corroborated Nick's, and the prosecution was off to an effective start. On the second day of the trial, the state introduced their third witness, David Freeman, whose account supported the stories of his two friends.

During cross-examination, Belge pressed Freeman to admit that Garrow was acting in a strange and erratic manner that day. It was an effort aimed at bolstering the defense claim of Garrow's insanity or mental instability.

The move backfired, leading instead to a tense exchange between the two. Freeman said the group had talked to Garrow and tried to calm him, after which Belge posed the question, "Was that because, in your opinion, Mr. Garrow was acting irrationally?"

Freeman shot back, "No, he was acting rational. He knew what he was doing." Belge continued, "I'm asking you, in your opinion, whether you consider it rational for a person to point a gun at you?" Freeman's response was, "Yes, in that instance."

Under questioning by Intemann, Freeman acknowledged that, when first confronted by Garrow in the tent, he believed the man wanted gas for his car. When asked what he now thought Garrow wanted that day, Freeman replied, "To murder the three of us and take my wife with him."

It was the perfect answer, concise and to the point. The prosecution called ten more people to the stand, but by the end of the afternoon session, Freeman proved to be the star witness of the day. His responses were featured prominently in news reports, and the next day's headlines proclaimed in some form or other that Garrow was rational. The defense team's initial effort to portray their client as a crazed killer was thwarted, perhaps in the eyes of the jury as well as the media.

On day three of the trial, a battle developed over several photographs offered as evidence by the prosecution. Because the pictures featured graphic depictions of the deceased victim, Belge took exception, noting that no one disputed the fact that Domblewski had died of stab wounds. He contended the pictures were offered for the sole purpose of inflaming the jury against the defendant.

The photographs in question were taken by Peter Knapick of the State Police Identification Unit. Knapick took the witness stand and underwent extensive questioning on all aspects of the photographs. Following his testimony, Judge Marthen overruled Belge's objection and allowed all eight items to be admitted as evidence.

Later on Wednesday, Belge garnered more attention by moving for a mistrial. He informed the court that the June 11 edition of the *Albany Times-Union* had been seen by some of the jurors, and claimed it contained a news item prejudicial against the defendant.

The story in question was about Harold E. Gormley, Jr., a decorated Vietnam War veteran who had pleaded guilty to four murders, including an execution-style triple murder at the Cabaret Lounge near South Glens Falls.

Since the trial's opening, Belge had frequently referred to his own client as "crazy," "a nut," and "irrational." The defense motion for mistrial was merely a continuance of the effort to suggest Garrow was insane.

Belge said the newspaper story about Gormley was "...a nut saying he is a nut," but any connection to Garrow's case appeared tenuous at best. Intemann argued that the story had absolutely no bearing on the trial at hand, and Judge Marthen agreed. The motion was denied.

During a week of testimony, the state called thirty-two witnesses, the last two of which appeared on Friday. At mid-morning, the prosecution rested its case. Judge Marthen then adjourned the trial until 10:00 a.m. on the following Monday, at which time Armani and Belge were expected to begin defense proceedings.

After the jury left the courtroom, Francis Belge moved for acquittal, claiming that "the evidence presented did not support the indictment." Intemann immediately objected, and Marthen denied the motion, ordering the defense to begin presenting its case when the court reconvened on Monday.

It would be a day none of them would soon forget.

6

Call Mr. Garrow!

At the next court session, prosecutors were allowed a few minutes to clarify some earlier testimony, after which Intemann stated, "At this time, your honor, the people rest."

Frank Armani asked for a brief recess to speak with his partner. Five minutes later, he and Belge returned to the courtroom, ready to proceed.

June 17, 1974, was a historic day in New York State criminal court. Robert Garrow's defense team presented its first witness at 10:20 a.m. Five and one-half hours later, all those in attendance had observed perhaps the most bizarre trial defense opening in the state's history.

Fifteen witnesses had been subpoenaed during the past week to testify on Garrow's behalf, and they were now prepared for duty. But three words, spoken loudly by defense attorney Francis Belge, stunned the courtroom: "Call Mr. Garrow!"

The judge was caught off guard, as were the prosecutors, the jury, spectators, and reporters. And so was Robert Garrow.

In Belge's assessment, the prosecution had spent five days building a powerful case against their client, and guilt or innocence was no longer the issue. The only hope for the defense was to prove Garrow was insane, the victim of some mental disease or defect that deprived him of the ability to separate right from wrong. Francis Belge had a plan to reveal Garrow's insanity, and it was time for action.

Since he was physically unable to access the witness box, Garrow's wheelchair was positioned in front of it. Judge Marthen issued the customary instructions before Belge commenced his questioning. Thus began an amazing journey through the dreadful life story of Robert Francis Garrow.

For the first three days of the case for the defense, he occupied the stand, repeatedly shocking listeners with details of his childhood. Then, as particulars of his adult life were revealed, Garrow's admissions of guilt to several major crimes generated revulsion, outrage, and uneasiness.

Among those to follow him in the witness chair were two of his sisters, his mother, and several psychiatrists, their testimony painting an incredible portrait of a dangerous killer. For the next ten days, trial attendees heard a tale that seemed improbable, if not impossible.

Readers across the country were held spellbound by the explicit accounts, and left uneasy in the knowledge that people like Robert Garrow walked among the general population.

Garrow's story and its analysis by professionals generated nearly two thousand pages of testimony. Some witnesses provided new segments of the story, or substantiated those already told. Others added insight, interpretation, or professional opinion. Together their stories wove a macabre tale disturbing to all.

Robert Francis Garrow was born in the town of Dannemora, New York on March 4, 1936, the son of Robert and Margaret Garrow. At the time of Robert's birth, the family address was given as Chazy Lake, New York, a small community several miles west of Dannemora village. The family's oral history indicates he was born in the Rand Hill section of Dannemora, and that the move to Chazy Lake came within a year or two of his birth.

Robert's father was Robert Omer Garrow, a Dannemora farmer, the son of Charles Garreau (Garrow) and Rosaline Arquette. His mother was Margarette Gebo of Altona, New York. Local records indicate she was the daughter of William Gebo and Emma Sharlou (also given as Sharland). However, her true parents almost certainly were Zephirin and Delia Gebo. Zephirin was William Gebo's brother.

Margarette's name sometimes appeared as Marguerite, but for most of her life, she went by Margaret. The confusion with names and family lines doesn't end there. Robert Omer Garrow had siblings who used the French spelling of the surname taken from their father, Charles Garreau, instead of the Anglicized version, Garrow.

Margaret Gebo, 16, and Robert Garrow, 20, were married in Dannemora on July 13, 1931. Their first child was Florence Mae, born on March 22, 1934. The birth record clearly states that Florence was Margaret's only living child, and her first-born.

Two years later, son Robert was born. Robert's birth record indicates he was the second child born to Margaret, and that she had only two living children.

Yet the family oral history suggests Florence and Robert were the second and third children of Margaret. Florence claimed to have an older brother living somewhere in the northern part of the state. That information came to the Garrow children from other relatives, and the family always believed it to be true.

There are many inconsistencies in the official records of the Gebo family. Margaret (Gebo) Garrow may well have married when she was barely fourteen years old. Her marriage certificate in 1931 noted Margaret's age as sixteen, indicating she was born in 1915.

However, when testifying in court in June 1974, Margaret said she was fifty-six, and would be fifty-seven before year's end. Twice she repeated her year of birth as 1917.

If her sworn testimony was accurate, Margaret had married when she was still thirteen, or right around her fourteenth birthday. Marrying at such a young age required written permission from a Family Court judge and both parents.

It was a bit easier for sixteen-year-olds, who only needed the signed consent of both parents. The record indicates that Margaret lied about her age, claiming she was sixteen, and it appears the "parents" who provided written consent were actually her aunt and uncle.

Such deceptions were not uncommon in birth and marriage records, and families usually had their reasons. In the case of Margaret Gebo, there is evidence to suggest she was pregnant at the time of her wedding. The further significance is that Margaret and Robert had two, and possibly three, children by the time she was just nineteen years old. Not exactly a template for success.

There is certainly some irony in Robert Garrow's place of

birth. Dannemora was home to Clinton State Prison (now the Clinton Correctional Facility), a maximum-security institution housing the state's most dangerous criminals. It is also home to all New York State prisoners on Death Row. Known locally as Dannemora Prison, for many decades it had a reputation for brutality. At Dannemora, hard time was the only time.

The prison grounds once housed the State Hospital for the Criminally Insane, informally and less delicately known as "the Bug House." The prison itself has long been referred to as "Little Siberia," a nod to both the seclusion of the area and the bitterly cold winters of the region. The village and the prison are located on the southern slope of Dannemora Mountain, at the upper northeastern rim of the Adirondack Mountains.

Around 1938, the Garrow family relocated briefly to North Hudson, and from there moved to Barton Hill at Mineville, where Mr. Garrow found employment in the iron mines.

Many of the homes in Mineville were in poor condition, and most families eked out a lower-class existence. On the day they moved in, young siblings Florence and Robert roamed the house with a hammer, using it to kill bedbugs and other critters.

The upbringing of the Garrow children was anything but normal. When they first moved to Mineville, new playmates were found among the other miners' families. But the new friends didn't last long. Margaret Garrow was a very unpleasant person, openly vulgar and disagreeable. After several encounters with other women, many of them learned to keep their distance.

In the words of her oldest daughter, Florence: "My mother was an extremely cruel person." When asked to describe her, Florence added, "My mother is approximately five-feet-five. She weighs approximately 380 pounds. She is a very strong woman and a brutal woman."

In the Garrow house, there were two rooms upstairs. One was used for storage, and the other served as the family bedroom. The children were severely punished if they made any reference to sex, yet Robert and Margaret frequently engaged in intercourse while the family was in the room.

Florence, Robert, and Agnes all testified that sexual activity often took place between their parents while the children were present. That arrangement continued for many years, until some of the children were in their early teens.

Margaret Garrow had a very foul mouth, frequently cursing, but that was one bad habit son Robert didn't pick up. Margaret seemed to enjoy the fact that her girth and demeanor scared or intimidated people, even her own children, and she used the effect to full advantage.

Young Robert had a chronic bedwetting problem for which his mother showed no mercy. She insisted a doctor had advised her to punish Robert in an effort to cure his condition. Alas, Margaret Garrow needed no prodding to punish her children.

About Robert's bedwetting, Florence recalled, "He always did. He was extremely nervous. My mother used to whip him all the time. Usually with anything she could get a hold of ... piece of stove wood, or anything. He always wore my clothes because of wetting. My mother used to make old-fashioned type bloomers with elastic over the knee, and he wore them."

The humiliating effect of forcing even a young boy to wear girls' clothing can be ego-shattering. But it was just one of many woeful examples of parenting in the Garrow household. Though the public embarrassment and the beatings didn't cure Robert's problem, Margaret didn't stop trying.

And it wasn't just Robert who felt her wrath, though he bore the brunt of it. The other children were also abused. Said Florence, "I had a very miserable home life, and my mother was an extremely cruel person." She added that all the children were treated the same, and that the child nearest at hand was often the one who took the abuse. Her parents argued constantly, and home life was wretched.

When she was still very young, Florence saw Robert receive many beatings. She recalled a leather strap with a metal buckle, and that both parts were used in the whippings.

Robert was frequently struck in the head, and Florence remembered at least one occasion where he was knocked unconscious after being picked up and thrown against the wall, something that didn't take much effort for a woman of Margaret's stocky, powerful build. Fearing he was dead, his sister threw water on Robert to revive him.

Of her father, Florence recalled seeing him leave for work with liquor bottles in his back pockets, a common practice among iron miners, many of whom drank as they worked. "My father was a very quiet man until he started drinking, which was almost every night, and he always drank Fitzgerald beer. If he didn't pick it up himself on the way home, my brother Bob and I used to take a little wagon, and we used to walk a good mile to get a case of Fitzgerald beer for him, and they used to charge it to my father at the little store."

Florence went on to relate a story about railroad ties, one that her mother later confirmed: "My mother used to have Bob and I and some of the other ladies on the hill pull them [the railroad ties] out when their husbands used to get drunk. The ties were put out into the road where the men were laying there drunk, so the cars wouldn't run over them."

Obviously, there was little in the way of role models in the Garrow household. Besides the beatings and whippings that were handed out for a variety of reasons, many others were given under false pretenses. Both Agnes and Florence recalled several instances where Robert was accused of stealing money from his father's pants.

Often it was Mrs. Garrow who had taken the money. But when confronted by her husband, she denied it, instead blaming the children. Almost invariably, it was Robert who was accused, and Robert who received a beating, even though he may not have stolen any money.

Agnes recalled one such occasion when a theft-related beating had been administered. Her mother then used the stolen money to buy some wine, which she drank in the back room, unbeknownst to her husband.

With constant abuse inflicted on the children, it took an especially egregious attack to stand out in memory. For young Robert, one of the worst was the cornfield incident. He was about seven years old, playing Hide-and-Seek in a cornfield, and some of the cornstalks were flattened.

Showing no mercy, Mr. Garrow beat him senseless, nearly ending his life with repeated kicks to the ribs. As Robert himself commented, "He almost killed me."

When he was around eight years old, an escape of sorts brought some relief to Robert from the terrible life in the Garrow household. Robert's father worked underground in the iron mines, in the Harmony Shaft, and had become friends with his boss. The supervisor's surname was of Slavic origin, but because he shared a farm locally with Mary Michalak, he was known to all as Stanley Michalak.

Besides the mining job, Mr. Garrow often worked on the farm, bringing his son along to help. The two men eventually came to an agreement that young Robert would be sent to live and work on the Michalak farm.

As Robert told it, he was put on the farm because the men were friends, but also because he was constantly in trouble at home with his parents. When Agnes and Florence spoke of their brother leaving for the farm, they always said their parents "gave Robert away" when he was very young.

He didn't work for free on the farm, but he didn't benefit financially early on. When Michalak brought Robert home on weekends, he paid Mr. Garrow for young Robert's services. It was an arrangement that lasted for many years.

Robert saw nearly nothing in wages for the first several years. As a teenager, he began receiving about twenty dollars per month, money that was used to purchase clothes and other necessities. Store-bought clothing was a rarity in the Garrow household, where most garments were assembled by Margaret.

By all accounts, the Michalaks were a very nice couple, and Robert was much happier on the farm than at home. He attended school regularly, and worked such long hours that he had little time to get into trouble. Best of all, for most of each week, he wasn't available for the regular beatings dished out by his parents.

Still, Robert had no one to associate with, and he did miss his sisters. Though he may have been "given away," as they saw it, the girls also noticed some of the advantages their brother enjoyed. Robert told them there was always plenty of food, and that he was treated well.

Eventually, both Florence and Agnes were hired by the Michalaks to help periodically with farm chores and housework.

They receive pay, but what they valued most was being treated with care and respect. It was difficult returning home to an atmosphere of abuse and parental neglect.

Though they envied Robert's happiness on the farm, what the girls didn't see was the tremendous workload placed on their brother's shoulders. Barely eight years old, he was already doing the job of a grown man.

Said Garrow, "I did everything on the farm from milking the cows, mowing hay, raking it up, collecting it, loading hay wagons, putting the hayforks in, getting the horses or the tractor, lifting it up, and putting it in the barn. I used to get up at three o'clock in the morning. I never used to hit the bed till eleven o'clock at night or so, and I did this for seven days a week all my life."

The Michalak farm was an extensive operation, including a full dairy, plus horses, turkeys, geese, ducks, and chickens. Some of the turkeys and chickens were raised for commercial purposes.

Corn for silage was produced, along with sweet corn, strawberries, potatoes, and barley as cash crops. Added Robert, "It was a big farm, and I had all the work to myself."

Attending school and working the farm kept him busy and out of trouble most of the time, but on the brief visits home, nothing had changed. The beatings continued, and Robert was still the main target.

Agnes recalls, "I know my father used a razor strap a lot. I remember my brother getting it, mostly. I used to run and hide. I remember there were times when he was punished by kneeling in the corner ... a long time, four or five hours."

Though the family had grown to include five children, it was the older girls who took the abuse during the week. The worst of the beatings occurred on the weekends, and at those times, Robert was the victim of choice.

Mr. Garrow's heavy drinking often made things worse. When he and Margaret weren't yelling or fighting, one of them could be found beating on Robert with a variety of household objects. The long hours working on the farm were still far preferable to such a hellish atmosphere.

The Michalaks, on the other hand, provided an opportunity

for normalcy. Despite such a terrible background at home for his first seven years, the responsibilities of working as a fulltime farmhand could well have been a turning point for a young man like Robert. A mix of discipline, experience, and duty often has that effect. But that is not what happened.

Instead, his life descended into a world of darkness and depravity. Life was better on the farm, but it was far from idyllic. For a troubled, misguided, and now unguided child, it became somewhat of a devil's playground.

Even at a very young age, Robert exhibited aberrant behavior on the Michalak farm. When asked on the witness stand about cows, horses, and other animals, he said, "I think the word they use today, with a woman you have intercourse. I used to have it with the animals ... when I was probably about ten, eleven, twelve years old. Of course, I used to fool around with the calves, too, you know."

His deviant behavior wasn't entirely secret, either. Robert described the surprise Mr. Michalak once received upon entering the barn. "I got caught one time. He walked in and seen me, and he walked away, and I paid no attention. He told me about it afterwards, not to do it anymore."

And it wasn't only animals. When asked about the barn equipment, he added, "I used to use the rubber cups on the milk machines the same as anyone would use a process to masturbate, and, I used to use the milk machine, if that answers your question."

Those were only the first of many shocking revelations jurors would hear. Left to his own devices at a young age, Robert regularly engaged in what is widely considered perverse, salacious behavior.

And the rest of his life was anything but normal. One particularly gruesome aspect of Robert's job was seldom handled by children, for obvious reasons. But, as the principal farmhand, he did it all, including the butchering.

Killing farm animals for food and other uses is as old as the bible itself, but the task is often very messy and traumatic. It is generally performed by adults, with younger observers gradually introduced to the practice. In most countries around the world, it is a fact of life and a matter of survival, but compared to modern processes, the old-style, hands-on methods are often considered barbaric.

By the age of eight, Robert Garrow was already intimately familiar with the process. "I used to help butcher pigs and so forth. In fact, when my father used to butcher them, I used to take a pan and I used to collect the blood for my mother to make blood pudding. You stick them in the neck, between the neck and the shoulders. My mother ... puts season in it and other stuff, and she makes the blood pudding, which I like. Then, after that, I used to do the butchering, after I seen how it was done."

While many people might cringe at that description, there is nothing unusual about it. Pretty much the same process is followed worldwide, both privately and commercially, to produce meat and meat byproducts, including blood pudding, for public consumption. Most people just prefer not to know the details. And most people don't allow children to perform what can often be a disturbing, distressing act.

But, barely eight years old, Robert had become the official executioner on an extensive farming operation. It wasn't just an occasional part of the job, but instead a frequent, violent duty. The potential harm to a child's psyche is obvious, though difficult to measure.

In Robert Garrow's case, here was an unloved child, frequently beaten, nearly always alone, and delving into the perverse practice of engaging in sex with various farm animals. Designated executioner was just the latest addition to an already miserable resume.

Robert explained to a rapt jury how he used various implements to complete the task of butchering, including a knife, a rifle, and a hammer to dispatch pigs, cows, ducks, and chickens. "Well, on the ducks I used to use a knife to cut off the top of their head to save the blood from them, because we used to make the old-fashioned Polish soup. [Duck's Blood Soup, or Czarnina, is a Polish favorite.—Editor.] I used to butcher all the calves, all the cows, the beefs, the bull."

He described an exceptionally difficult killing that took place when he was around ten years old. The object of attention was one of Michalak's bulls. "I had a .38-40 Winchester lever action that belonged to my father. It's a heavy-grain shell. I couldn't kill it with the rifle ... the lead kept bouncing off its skull, so finally, I had to get a twenty-pound sledgehammer, and I had to hit it.

"It would just go down to its knees, so I got all the madder and hit it again, kept on hitting it, and finally ... I knocked it unconscious. We pulled it on a pulley gizmo and all that, and then we sliced the necks to butcher 'em."

Watching Robert kill the bull were his father and Mr. Michalak. "I did the skinning. They were drinking beer. They were having a ball."

When asked if the slaughter of the bull upset him, he replied, "No, I enjoyed it, because I used to like the blood. I used to drink it because it's good for you. And I got the hide for doing it." Courtroom observers fairly cringed at the mental images induced by the accused killer's comments, delivered in matter-of-fact fashion.

The Michalaks sold meat to individuals and local concerns, including the restaurant and tavern owned by Mary's three sons. The slaughtering business kept Robert very busy.

"I did it all for the Michalak's Tavern down in Ticonderoga. I used to get about three dollars for the hides, and that is where I got a few pennies. I salted the hide and sold it to hide dealers. I did all the butchering and everything, and the innards from the calves and cows I used to dump in the pigpen for the pigs to demolish.

"I started when I was nine years old. I started with the young stock, young heifers, veal we called them. They are about seven or eight or nine weeks old. We used to butcher them for the restaurant."

When defense attorney Belge questioned Garrow on the particulars of his butchering duties, it seemed an obvious attempt to further shock jurors with the grisly details. But Belge's city lifestyle may have betrayed him, causing him to misjudge his most important audience.

The average person on the jury was sixty-two years old. They were all lifetime residents of the most rural county in the state, and well familiar with most of the practices described by Robert Garrow. Except, of course, for drinking the blood.

Still, it was clear that such gruesome duties were best left to adults, and unthinkable for such a troubled young child. Robert's youth thus far had been one of seclusion, long hours of heavy labor, the violent dispatching of farm stock, and intense abuse at the hands of his parents.

His single respite from it all came when Robert attended school. Other than that, he only saw his sisters briefly, either on weekend visits or at Sunday morning mass, which was attended by most miners' families. Occasionally he visited with Florence and Agnes when they hired on to help the Michalaks with farm duties and housework.

With all of the intense physical work his job required, Robert became strong beyond his years, even as a young child. He also became less accepting of the beatings dished out by his parents, and at any sign of rebellion, he was struck down harshly.

At about the age of twelve, he decided he'd had enough. A nephew of the Michalak's had returned from military service, and among his possessions was a pistol. Robert seized the opportunity, stealing the gun with the intent of using it to kill his parents.

When he discovered the gun was inoperable (the firing pin had been removed), he confided his failed plan to Florence, who was shaken by the disclosure, but dared not tell her parents. In a home already rife with turmoil, there was no telling how they might react.

During pre-trial psychiatric examinations, Garrow described the plan to kill his parents, noting that he heard "whispers" in his ears for the first time. He couldn't make out what words the whispers were saying, but it was an event he later claimed occurred often in his adult life, immediately prior to the commission of various crimes.

As he reached his teen years, Robert was sometimes outright rebellious. He once left the Michalak farm for several weeks, only to be ordered back by his parents because he couldn't get along at home with the family. Prosecutors suggested a different scenario: that he was sent home by the Michalaks after being accused of stealing money and jewelry from them. Garrow insisted he had only been accused of stealing the revolver.

After nearly eight years of working on the farm, Robert finally returned home when the Michalaks decided to rent the property to a German couple. Nearly sixteen years old, he was a strapping, dangerously maladjusted boy with frightening capabilities. When his father resorted to the customary abusive treatment of his son, the two of them faced off in several violent, vicious encounters.

Two major incidents at this time brought great change to Garrow's life. The first occurred when he neglected to milk the family cow, an offense that landed an iron bar across his head, courtesy of his enraged father.

As Robert told it, "I didn't milk it, so he attacked me with a crowbar ... he hit me with it, and I grabbed him, and grabbed the crowbar. It pushed me in the snow bank, and my mother got in between us and she called the state police."

Another time, Robert came home with some berries and asked Agnes to make him some muffins. There wasn't enough flour in the house, and contrary to the wishes of his mother, Robert went to borrow some flour from a neighbor.

Said Agnes, "My mother didn't want him to ... but he did anyway. My father came home in his drunken condition. She started telling him, and he took the strap to Robert. My brother stood up to defend for himself, and they got into a fistfight. My mother got in between and got accidentally punched, and they blamed him for it. He was sent to reform school. They accused him of punching her."

As a result of those two instances, and with the consent of his wife, Mr. Garrow went to a Ticonderoga justice and had Robert committed to the State Industrial School at Rochester. After sixteen years, they were unable to control him physically, and he was no longer useful to them. He now belonged to the state.

The grand title of State Industrial School was simply a euphemism for reform school, many of which were dismal failures. The intent was to introduce discipline and structure into the lives of troubled youths, but results were mixed at best.

To avoid the stigma of being branded as criminals in youth lockups, the attendees were called juvenile delinquents, and the institutions were called schools. The general view was more simply stated: they were basically prisons for kids.

The State Industrial School at Rochester underwent many transformations over the years. When Garrow arrived, it was known officially as the State Agricultural and Industrial School. In its latest incarnation, it was considered a cottage reformatory, and was a typical youth penal institution of that era.

Across the grounds of New York's best-known reform school were twenty cottages, each accommodating twenty-five boys, or inmates. They slept in two large dormitories, had regimented group calisthenics, and attended daily classes.

During the time that Robert was there, the focus of the work program was on agriculture. Moral guidance was provided by a husband-and-wife team of guardians assigned to each cottage. Sincere efforts were made to help, but these were some very tough cases from all walks of life.

Garrow's farming experience indicated that an agricultural program might be a good fit for him, and just the change he needed. But with a background like Robert's, he would never fit well anywhere.

7

A Life of Crime

About a year after he was committed, Robert was removed from the State Industrial School by Florence, who lived in nearby Buffalo. Mr. and Mrs. Garrow only learned of his departure when one of their monthly payments of $5 was returned, accompanied by the explanation that their son was no longer at the institution.

At that same time, another family member ran into trouble with the law. Robert's grandfather, Charles Garrow, seventy-one years old, was arrested and subsequently convicted of endangering the morals of a child. He was placed under strict probationary supervision and ordered to undergo psychiatric testing. Charles' grandson would one day find himself in very similar circumstances.

Now seventeen years old and living with Florence and her husband, Robert found work producing mirrors in a glass factory, but lost the job within a month after getting into what he termed "a scrape."

Next, he found employment at Buffalo's Pillsbury factory, remaining there for about eight months. In January 1954, barely a month shy of his eighteenth birthday, Garrow joined the air force. Clearly, he was a very troubled, unstable young man who might benefit from the strict guidance and discipline of life in the service.

He had never dated girls, and on a train en route to basic training, Robert claimed to have experienced his first kiss, but didn't offer details as to the circumstances. At another time, it was referred to as his first sexual experience. If so, considering Robert's description of similar events in later life, it is not implausible that there might have been criminal elements to the encounter.

In a first-rate example of irony, Garrow was assigned to the Air Police Squadron, what many people know better as a branch of the military police. His initial placement as an MP was no doubt the high point of a less than distinguished service record.

Robert's time in the military did not go well. The enuresis (bedwetting) that had always plagued him as a child was still prevalent, and it made him a constant source of ridicule. A bedwetting civilian might be able to hide the problem, but that just wasn't possible in the military. For a young man entering adult life, the shame and embarrassment were enormous.

He also managed to get himself into legal difficulties, an overriding theme in his life. As Robert told it, "I got in trouble in [the] service, also. Well, I used to have dirty pictures and sell them, and so forth, and I got in trouble with a friend of mine. We took a camera. We hocked it to get some money to go out."

The camera in question was the property of his sergeant, and criminal charges were brought against Garrow. He was convicted of theft and sentenced to six months in military prison at Eglin Air Force Base in Florida.

Not at all enthralled with confinement, Garrow successfully escaped incarceration, but was recaptured and sentenced to an additional year in the stockade at Fort Gordon, Georgia. He served his time, and upon release, was given a discharge from the military for enuresis and an inability to adjust to military life. Since leaving Buffalo eighteen months earlier, Garrow had spent most of his air force career in prison.

Departing Georgia and the military in June 1955, Robert went once again to live with Florence, who had moved to Albany, New York. Along the shores of the Hudson River in Troy, he found work at Railway Express during the Christmas rush, operating a small tractor hauling long wagons of mail unloaded from the rail cars.

When the holiday season ended, Robert was laid off. After a few odd jobs, including one at a small bakery, he found part-time work at Hot Shoppes, a restaurant chain that later grew to become Marriott International.

At Hot Shoppes, Robert found more trouble. After leaving the restaurant for other employment, he returned to collect wages that were missing from his severance pay. At issue were expenses incurred when he had cut his finger on the job, requiring emergency room treatment. According to the manager, the money was withheld to cover hospital charges, but that didn't satisfy Robert.

In late February 1956, a couple of months after he left Hot Shoppes, Garrow paid a visit to the restaurant and spoke with his former boss. The manager restated the company's position as he took the day's proceeds and locked them in a safe. For Garrow, the meeting became phase one of a revenge plan.

At 2:30 the next morning, Robert returned for phase two. "I went back there at night to get the paycheck out of the drawer, and it wasn't there, so I got mad and I just tore the place up. The police got me the next day, I guess. I tore the whole thing up, the whole office. I even pushed the desk over. I pushed the safe over."

Describing his arrest, Garrow recounted the efforts by Albany police to obtain a signed statement. "First they started out by buying me a cup of coffee, and then they got me at the stairs. They pushed me down the stairs, and they brought me back up. I still refused to sign it, and they dropped the typewriter on my foot. I did sign that statement. I recall it now."

Garrow was arrested and held in the Albany County Jail. He had problems there, too, brawling with other inmates and suffering a severe cut to the head, requiring two days of treatment in an Albany hospital. There was sufficient concern about his behavior to have a psychiatrist assigned to his case, delving into the reasons behind his unruly actions.

Though he was convicted on the break-in charges, Robert's court-appointed attorney managed to get him released on probation. He remained in the city for a time, and Railway Express offered him another job driving truck north of the Albany area. Garrow turned it down because he had never possessed a driver's license. He had been driving for years without one.

Eventually, the attorney gave him $25 for train fare so he could return to Mineville. There, as his father had done long ago, Robert went to work in the mines for Republic Steel Corporation. He considered boarding with his parents, but when they demanded he surrender his entire paycheck, he rented a room for twenty dollars a week from a family in Witherbee.

After working for Republic Steel for about eight months, he became unemployed again in July when the miners went on strike. The men returned to work three weeks later, but by that time, Robert had taken a job driving truck for the O.C. Buck Show, a traveling carnival operation.

Operated by Oscar Buck of Troy, the O.C. Buck Show was an annual summer attraction across the Adirondack region, setting up and tearing down each week as they moved from town to town. Robert drove a tractor-trailer rig and performed many other tasks as the carnival traveled north in the summer of 1956.

In the Ogdensburg area, while operating the large Ferris wheel, Robert was hospitalized after being struck on the head by one of the swinging chairs. Changing jobs again, he found employment with the D.A. Collins Construction Company, running a jackhammer on a bridge crew. Later, he turned to work that was much more familiar, hiring on as a farmhand near Lowville, south of Watertown.

The operation was a dairy farm, perhaps a little larger than the Michalak's. He maintained his powerful work ethic, but Robert also admitted to resuming unsavory habits from his earlier farming days, engaging in repeated acts of bestiality.

While in Lowville, Robert met and became friends with Edith Foster, a local telephone operator, and his future wife. When he was laid off from the farm job, he went to live with Edith while seeking employment in the surrounding communities.

After finding work at another farm, Robert managed to land in trouble once again. He was arrested on suspicion of larceny, convicted, and sentenced to Lewis County Jail for thirty days. During his incarceration there, it was discovered he was wanted in Albany for violation of probation. After completing his Lewis County sentence, he was turned over to Albany police to face charges there.

The probation violation stemmed from Robert's nomadic life style after leaving Mineville, where he had regularly received forms from the probation office. While he drifted from job to job across the northern Adirondacks, the forms continued

Robert Francis Garrow, Sr.

Top: Freeman and Malinowski's tent, where they were abducted by Garrow near Speculator. Middle: Typical view of searchers during the manhunt. Bottom: Garrow's car, abandoned after chase by NYS Troopers. Branches still dangle from the car window. All photos, 1973. (Syracuse Newspapers Photo Library)

Top: Searching car trunks at a roadblock in the town of Wells (1973). Middle: Roadblock on Route 84 near Fishkill after Garrow's escape (1978). Bottom: Garrow's body is removed following the shootout near Fishkill Correctional Facility (1978). (Syracuse Newspapers Photo Library)

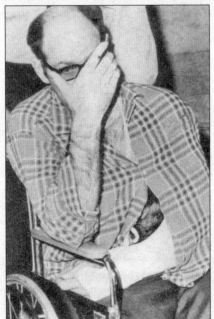

For all the attention and publicity he received, Garrow rarely showed his face for the cameras. Occasionally he slipped up, but aside from the police mug shots, he effectively foiled most photographers. (Syracuse Newspapers Photo Library)

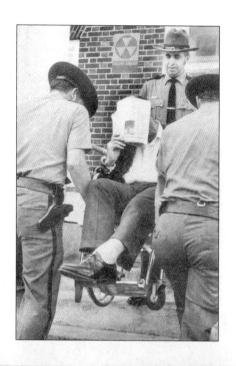

The many homes away from home of Robert Garrow. Top: Dannemora Prison, circa 1936. Middle: the grounds of the State Agricultural and Industrial School (reform school) near Rochester. Bottom: a sample of the military-style regimen at the school, including daily group exercise.

Top: on the right is the Hamilton County Courthouse. To the left of the courthouse, behind the flagpole, is the former Hamilton County Jail that housed Garrow during his trial. Middle: Fishkill Correctional Facility. Bottom: Auburn Correctional Facility.

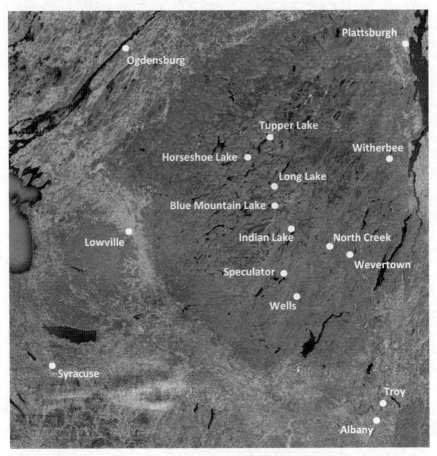

North Country Nightmare

Albany – parole violation, robbery, rape, assaults, abductions, sexual assaults
Horseshoe Lake – spent night, went through Blue Mountain Lake and Long Lake
Indian Lake – ran roadblock, escaped high-speed chase
Lowville – farming job; met future wife; jailed 30 days for larceny
North Creek – gas station encounter with Betty Baker
Ogdensburg – hospitalized with head injury when struck by Ferris Wheel seat
Plattsburgh – hospitalized after being shot and captured at Witherbee
Speculator – two attempted abductions of young girls, stole car, escaped chase
Syracuse – abductions, child sexual assaults, six rapes, murder of Alicia Hauck
Troy and Albany – years of deviant sexual trysts with lawyer and companion
Wells – abduction of four campers, murder of Philip Domblewski
Wevertown – murdered Daniel Porter, abducted Susan Petz
Witherbee – abused, raped, and murdered Susan Petz; later, shot and captured

accumulating at Mineville, finally generating a warrant for his arrest. Garrow claimed he had tried contacting the office twice, but received no reply. That led him to conclude his probation period had ended.

Perhaps it wasn't the best of defense arguments, but it was sufficient for his attorney to once again secure Robert's release from jail. For the second time, he also helped him out financially.

This time, though, Garrow's lawyer went much further than just providing cash for travel expenses. He allowed Robert to move into the home he shared with his mother, and gave him some spending money. Eventually, he secured a job for Robert at Williams Press in Menands, found an apartment for him, and bought pots, pans, dishes, and other items for his new place.

The Albany attorney was beginning to sound like someone with a social conscience, really trying to make a difference. Any notion of altruism was soon dispelled.

During questioning by Francis Belge about his former attorney, Robert stopped short of providing details, and then asked, "You don't want me to go into the rest, do you? It's embarrassing, you know." Belge urged him to continue.

"The people refer today, like a 'fairy,' you like to play with boys. And I had a good build, husky build, and he started by taking pictures of me in his basement. He used to wear jockey shorts. In other words, he started in gradual, I didn't know it at the time, but as a year goes by you realize this.

"And then it got down to where we got out in the woods. He had a timed camera, used to take pictures, and used to have me, well, he used to have me play with him, et cetera, and so forth, you know."

That behavior continued for a few years, even following his marriage to Edith in June 1957, when Robert was twenty-one years old. He also testified that, after they married, Edith became the first female he ever had intercourse with. Until then, he either masturbated or engaged in sex with various animals.

Seeking different employment, Garrow left Williams Press and found work as an electrician for Charles Rappazzo, an Albany electrical contractor. In addition, he did many side jobs around the neighborhood. Whether the work required carpentry, electrical, or other skills, Robert considered himself an able jack-of-all-trades.

Though he was married and working different jobs, Garrow's deviant sexual relationship with the attorney expanded. Psychiatrists who later examined him classified the behavior as homoerotic sadomasochistic activities. Garrow was at times tied up, and photographs were taken of him having sexual relations with a woman who may have been the attorney's wife. He was also frequently beaten with a whip.

Though she didn't know about it for certain, Edith suspected something was going on, and she wasn't alone. Detectives once asked about the scars on his back, and his boss, Rappazzo, had also once seen them, according to Garrow.

The odd liaisons continued well after he was married, suddenly ending in late 1961 with Robert's arrest on very serious criminal charges. In November of that year, he used a pellet pistol and a knife in the abduction of a young Albany area football player and his girlfriend.

After seeing the couple out walking together, Garrow hurried home to get his gun. Returning to the scene, he guided them to a secluded area, beat the boy into semi-consciousness, tied him with shoestrings, and raped the girl. The rope-and-rape strategy would become his routine modus operandi.

Two days later, police attempted to arrest Robert, but he did not surrender easily. As lawmen approached, he ran, and the ensuing chase was like something from a gangster film of the 1930s. Several shots were fired, and Garrow was finally captured. The spectacular story made great headline fodder for local papers, but there was more to come.

While in police custody on charges including assault, rape, robbery, and resisting arrest, Robert came under suspicion in a recent unsolved case involving another sexual attack. He was soon identified as the perpetrator, having committed an equally horrific crime less than two weeks earlier.

In late October, Garrow had used a gun to abduct two thirteen-year-old girls, claiming he was a police officer. He took them to a wooded hillside, where he raped one of the girls, forcing the other to hold the girl's mouth closed so she couldn't scream.

The two were held prisoner for more than eight hours.

No one will ever know if it was the first time Garrow committed such horrible acts, or if it was just the first time he had been caught. A psychiatrist years later speculated that the twisted relationship with his attorney may have led Garrow to act out his fantasies in criminal fashion. Perhaps the doctor was unaware of his patient's already extensive background of crime, violence, and perversion.

Whatever the case, Robert Garrow was obviously a dangerous man, and out of control. Facing a trial and almost certain conviction in Albany, he accepted a plea bargain worked out by his attorney. Garrow admitted guilt to one count of rape in satisfaction of all charges.

The judge pronounced a sentence of ten to twenty years, and, in an ironic sense, the twenty-five-year-old was going home. He was exiled to serve his time in Dannemora, Robert Garrow's birthplace, and home to the very worst of New York State's violent criminals.

When Robert went to prison, he was already the father of two small children, a son and a daughter. Edith moved the family from Albany to Syracuse, about thirty miles east of Auburn State Prison. Garrow served two years of his sentence at Dannemora, during which time he and Edith wrote letters to the commissioner of Auburn, petitioning for a transfer.

The move was granted, and Robert soon found himself within easy visiting range of his family. Unknown to all at the time, Robert's familiarity with the transfer process would serve him well in the future.

When asked about any sex that may have occurred while he was in prison at both Dannemora and Auburn, Garrow said, "Yes, I had a job in the gallery, with the water boy, after hours. So, you know. The galleries are long, you know, in prison, and there's no guards. There's only two guards in the whole block, and the block is several stories high."

Asked about what type of sex they engaged in, he answered, "Well, I guess they refer to it as sodomy. Both of them—oral and anal."

Garrow also kept very busy in other ways while in prison,

availing himself of many learning opportunities. He described for the court his varied schooling, a lengthy list of items worth repeating. It included ICS correspondence courses; a Dale Carnegie course; many levels of algebra, trigonometry, and calculus; training to use an engineer's slide rule; typing; violin lessons; English; radio and television construction and repair; theology; and a course on the Knights of Columbus.

When discussing the theology course, Robert stated his belief in god, stemming from his upbringing as a Roman Catholic since early childhood. When asked if he knew the Ten Commandments, and if he knew specifically the Fifth Commandment, "Thou shalt not kill," Garrow replied, "Yes, sir, I sure do. I had to write an essay on it for Father Breinneger at Woodstock College."

The irony of the moment was not lost on court spectators.

There seemed to be a danger in Belge's strategy of exposing the jury to Garrow's extensive schooling. In the mind of the average person, it is difficult to reconcile advanced education with supposed depravity and insanity. It is also important to note that the tutelage Garrow described would one day prove critical to his future.

Although it has been frequently mentioned that he served eight years in prison, the statement is misleading. Garrow did serve time in each of the eight years from 1961-68, but his actual time in prison was about six and a half years.

In August 1968, the New York State parole board deemed him fit for release, and he went to live with Edith and their two children in Syracuse. There, Robert found work at the Interstate Brand Corporation, a major player in the baking industry. His duties involved repairing and maintaining machinery, and he eventually became a first-class mechanic.

Up to that point, Garrow's life had been anything but normal, and in time, the pattern resumed in Syracuse. As he explained it, "For the first couple of years I got along good at home, but any time when I did something and my wife used to say I'm wrong, I used to get big, you know, pressure started building up, and I walked away. I don't know where I would go or where I had been."

That statement summarized Robert's personal defense for

all the wrongs he had committed. During his lengthy testimony regarding several monstrous deeds, there was one dominant assertion: none of it was his fault. Pressure wrought anger, anger caused him to perpetrate criminal acts, and the crimes caused partial amnesia, leaving Garrow blissfully ignorant of all that had occurred.

Literally hundreds of times, he alluded to a lack of self-awareness while committing vile acts, and thus had no actual memory of having done so. Instead, he claimed it was his remarkable analytical skills that later reconstructed the missing portions of his life. Nearly every time Robert spoke more than a few sentences in court, there came a reminder that he had "put the pieces together."

He described intense anxiety, mental pressures, and severe headaches, usually associated with a disturbing personal problem. During those troubled times, Garrow would disappear for hours, and sometimes for days. He often returned home feeling refreshed, but with no recollection of recent events, which invariably included criminal activities.

Later, while perusing the newspapers, he or Edith might notice articles about crimes in which the description of the assailant matched Robert's appearance. He then "put the pieces together," and concluded he had committed the offense in question while he had been "away."

On other occasions, Garrow said he learned details of crimes while undergoing interrogation by lawyers or investigators. Then, possibly months later, fragmented recollections surfaced, matching what he had learned during questioning. He often remembered trivial details of life from those periods, but inexplicably, his memory failed during those moments when he was committing crimes.

He stuck to that explanation religiously through three full days of testimony, repeating the "pieces" theme ad nauseam. The court record is replete with it. Perhaps it was more believable when spoken before a jury, but when the written record is examined, the effect is quite different. It comes across as a transparent tactic that was nothing other than self-serving.

But Robert had scammed many people throughout life, and

he never stopped trying. His piecemeal memory was a wonderful, all-purpose alibi that excused him from responsibility for the most heinous of acts.

In the case of the attack on the young boy and girl near Albany in 1961, Garrow claimed the impetus arose from an argument with Edith. Angry with her, he had destroyed her new dress, torn up their marriage certificate, and was searching for the checkbook. Upon learning she had hidden it, Robert became so incensed that he left the house.

Two days later, detectives picked him up for questioning in the assault of the young athlete and the rape of his girlfriend. Garrow said police then beat him in order to get a confession, but he refused to sign a statement.

When Belge inquired if he remembered doing it at the time, Garrow shook his head no. When asked if he remembered it now, he replied, "Yes, the whole detail. There was a guy also with her, and I supposedly knocked him out with a rabbit punch. I don't know what a rabbit punch is. I still don't know what it is. I went to jail. It was for quite a while, eight years, I guess, all told."

In Syracuse, the return of the amnesia episodes meant it was possible Garrow was once again "unknowingly" committing serious crimes. There may have been many other odious offenses during those first two years, but none to which he had been positively linked.

During questioning, Belge prodded Robert to recount his first criminal act after being released from prison and moving to Syracuse. The request surprised him, as well as the entire courtroom. Was his own defender asking Garrow to admit crimes he had never been accused of?

As it turned out, that was exactly Belge's strategy, a risky attempt at proving his client's mental instability. After all, who else but an insane person would offer evidence of his own guilt in a series of brutal crimes?

Urged to continue, Robert said, "I guess you'd call it rape. That's the term they use today. But at the time ... I guess it happened the second year after I was home. Listen, nobody knows about this, though, just the doctors. You're putting me in a spot here, though. You know that. You put me in a spot."

Reporters, spectators, jurors, and prosecutors alike were stunned. A man on trial for murder was sitting before them, admitting to a heretofore undisclosed rape. Perhaps the same thought was on everyone's mind. What could Belge hope to accomplish by such tactics?

Adding drama to the moment, Garrow abruptly began sobbing, and Frank Armani sprang to his feet to halt the proceedings. A tense exchange followed as Belge insisted he be allowed to continue, while Armani protested in favor of a recess. Interestingly, one defense lawyer was raising objections against the other, while the prosecution sat idly by.

As the legal partners disagreed, Garrow interrupted to say he would press forward. It all happened suddenly, but Judge Marthen quickly took control, ordering everyone to be quiet.

When calm was restored, the court allowed a twenty-minute recess for Garrow to compose himself. There would be many similar breakdowns throughout his testimony, some during questioning by his own attorneys, and some during cross-examination by prosecutors. Norman Mordue would elicit more than his share of tears from the defendant.

With everyone once again seated in the courtroom, Garrow was reminded by Judge Marthen that he was not required to give any incriminating testimony. Robert asked if doing so would cause him to be treated any differently while held in jail. Marthen said no, but explained that if Robert offered information on other crimes, he was exposing himself to further prosecution.

Garrow decided to continue with the rape story, insisting he had been raised to tell the truth, and therefore had no choice. He asked the judge directly if he could answer the questions as he saw fit. Marthen assured him that plenty of latitude would be allowed.

With that, Robert began with a bluntness that fairly took the jury's breath away. "I went out and had incest with a broad. I had a little argument with my wife that night and I just went out and that was it. I didn't know anything about it until two days later, though. I read about it in the papers.

"It happened at the park. I should say on Spencer Street it happened. There was a piece in the paper about it. And my wife said I wasn't home that night, and that's when it dawned on me, you know. In other words, I had the ability of putting pieces together because I was trained that way."

When asked what he meant by incest, and if it was by force, he said, "I had intercourse with her. Yes, you could call it force." He said the victim was likely in her mid-twenties.

According to prosecutors, in June 1970, Garrow had used a pistol to force a young girl and her boyfriend towards Spencer Street and then down by the barge canal. There, he raped the girl and forced her to perform oral sex on him, all the time holding the gun on the boyfriend and making him watch.

When later confronted with that story during cross-examination, Garrow's response was adamant: "No sir. ... I know nothing about that ... I'm not saying I don't recall it. I didn't do it, period."

Amidst frequent claims of memory loss, Garrow's sudden lucidity about crime details from four years earlier didn't do much for his credibility. It instead made his memory lapses seem quite convenient.

Belge continued the same line of questioning, and Garrow once again shocked the courtroom: "Out in the park one time, this broad was ... Schiller Park, I think they call it, because I used to take my daughter swimming there.

"And she was in a car, she was naked with another guy on top of her, and I opened the door, and of course I used language, telling them I was a park patrol or something, and so on, and so forth, and scared the guy off, and took her in the park, and I had intercourse with her. I don't know her name. I don't know any of their names."

Garrow may have been confused somewhat about dates, but police had records of the attacks he described, and statements from the victims. This particular crime occurred in September 1969, barely a year after his release from prison.

The seventeen-year-old victim said she was near the pool in Schiller Park with her boyfriend when a man showed a card to her, identifying himself as a police officer. He told the boy to leave, and then raped the girl. The card in question was believed to be Robert's prison photo I.D.

Garrow had now admitted to two rapes, but Belge wasn't finished, prodding his client to continue. A third rape was confirmed, this one also taking place in Schiller Park in Syracuse.

In August 1971, a young couple was "parking" in the same area by the pool. Garrow tied the girl's right hand to the boy's hand and took them to a more secluded area of the park. There, he forced the boy to lie down while Garrow raped the girl. Or, as he preferred to say, "I had intercourse with her."

People in the courtroom were mortified at what they were hearing. After relating the details of a horrible childhood and a bizarre sex life, Garrow was revealing a string of rapes and sexual assaults. And there was more.

"The next time it happened was in the cemetery, not too far from where I lived. I think the cemetery is called Morningdale Cemetery, or something like that. It was my day off. Of course, I wanted to leave the house. I couldn't sleep all that night. I just had to get out, so after I got a few Excedrin and Alka-Seltzer, I left the house and went up to the cemetery.

"This girl was supposedly walking down, walking up, and I supposedly had a gun, which was a cap gun, and we marched off in the bushes, and so forth, and we had intercourse.

"I didn't know about it till the next day, when my wife seen it in the papers, 'A guy with red shirt and a hat,' and so on, and so forth. My wife showed it to me, and that's when it dawned on me, because my wife even said it, it just fits me perfectly, the description. As I said again, I had that knack of putting pieces together. I took the blame for it. I don't know if I did it or not, I still don't know, but I still took the blame for it."

By taking the blame for it, Garrow simply meant he assumed he was responsible. Until his testimony in 1974, he had not admitted any crimes since the Albany attacks in 1961.

Belge challenged him, saying, "Come on, you know you did it. Stop putting us on," to which Garrow replied, "It's not putting you on. It's the truth. In other words, what I mean is, at the time, I didn't know I did it."

Garrow was later pressed by prosecutor Norman Mordue for details on the cemetery attack, prompting an exchange that highlighted Robert's spotty memory:

MORDUE: In June of 1972, on a Thursday, about 11:50 in the morning, do you recall being over in the cemetery [near Garrow's home] when a seventeen-year-old girl came through? This is where you had on your maroon shirt, and hat, glasses.

GARROW: I had intercourse with her. [I had] a cap gun. We went up in the woods and right there in the cemetery, we had intercourse.

MORDUE: Isn't it a fact that you took the girl, grabbed her at gunpoint, tied her to a tree, and raped her?

GARROW: I don't remember her being tied to no tree. How can you rape a girl tied to a tree?

MORDUE: Because you tied her loosely to a tree. Well, did you have intercourse with her?

GARROW: Yes.

MORDUE: Were her hands tied to the tree?

GARROW: No.

MORDUE: If she stated that, that would be a lie, right?

GARROW: No, I can't say it because I don't remember it that good.

Besides addressing the issue of Garrow's convenient memory lapses, the exchange also touched on two recurring themes in his crimes; the use of trees, and tying up his victims. Jurors might wonder if an insane man possessed the wherewithal to repeatedly use such a planned, controlled process on a plethora of victims spanning more than a decade.

As the story unfolded, another chilling truth emerged. Contrary to earlier reports, Garrow had not been a model parolee after his release in 1968. Instead, he was a monster unleashed on an unsuspecting citizenry.

No arrests had been made in the four rape incidents Garrow described. Syracuse police were constantly on the alert, but the perpetrator had proven to be an elusive target, and officials were forced to play a waiting game. With the frequency of attacks, it seemed likely the offender would eventually slip up.

It finally happened in late 1972 when Robert was arrested for kidnapping a pair of Syracuse University students. Possession of drugs was added to the charges when marijuana was found in his car.

These were very serious accusations for a man with a felony record and time served in two maximum-security lockups. If Garrow had been held in violation of parole, he may well have ended up back in prison. Many other crimes would not have been committed, and Philip Domblewski would still be alive.

But luck was again on Garrow's side in outlandish fashion. The legal system served the criminal, and several innocent citizens soon paid the horrific consequences.

Few specifics of the story involving the students had been made public, but through direct testimony and tough defense questioning, frightening details emerged.

The incident in question happened in mid-November, in the early morning hours just after midnight. Two students, one male and one female, were hitchhiking near the university, and Garrow picked them up. The young man took the front seat, and the girl sat in back.

Garrow drove them around for a while, then parked the orange Volkswagen in the Skytop area of Syracuse and took out his pistol. Sticking the barrel of the gun into the man's mouth, Robert promised to blow his brains out if he tried anything.

After forcing the girl to tie the young man, Garrow did the same to the girl, and told her she would have to watch while he worked her friend over. He took to the road once more, with two frightened victims wondering what ghastly fate awaited them.

But whatever nefarious plans Garrow had were soon thwarted. The girl succeeded in untying her ropes and began beating furiously on Robert as he drove. The young man also freed himself, and together they managed to escape the vehicle and called police. Left behind, under the back seat, was a small bag of marijuana.

Based on information provided by the two students, Garrow was identified as their abductor. When his car was searched by police, Robert was asked if he owned everything in the vehicle. When he confirmed it was all his property, the officers produced the bag of marijuana, and a drug offense was added to the kidnapping charges.

Garrow was jailed, but Armani soon secured his freedom on bail. It appeared at first that Robert was in significant trouble for the abduction, and his lawyer would have a tough time preventing his return to prison.

Eventually, the attorney's investigation determined that the bag of marijuana actually belonged to the students. Armani now possessed powerful leverage, and he exercised it on behalf of his client.

When the case finally went before a judge in April 1973, the students had changed their minds about pressing charges. Considering the situation, and the trouble they might be in for possession of drugs, both agreed not to prosecute.

During final resolution of the case, the judge lauded Garrow's clean record since leaving prison in 1968. He noted that Robert had been framed by the two students, and that releasing him from custody would right a miscarriage of justice.

Instead of a dangerous repeat offender, the accused was a shining example of success for New York State's correctional system. Frank Armani had done his homework, and Robert Garrow was a free man.

Francis Belge now guided Garrow's testimony forward in time to his most recent trouble in the Syracuse area. On May 31, 1973, he had gone to the city's western suburb of Geddes and abducted two young girls. Robert told them he was a policeman looking for a lost dog, and that he would take the girls to the police station to help him.

Instead, he drove to Camillus, several miles from Geddes. Parking in a secluded area, he took them to a wooded hillside. As Garrow told the court, "We didn't go to the top of the hill. I was still on the hill. I think there was one of the girls that took her dress off, or lifted it up, if that will help you any, and I had the girls play with me ... and one of them committed an act of sodomy, orally, and that is what happened. Just the one of them. The other girl, I had her play with me."

When prosecutor Mordue later confronted Garrow about the young girls, he said, "And you attempted to have intercourse with the nine-year-old, didn't you. You actually tried to penetrate that girl."

Garrow simply answered, "No." Contrary to his putting the pieces together, Robert's memory suddenly seemed clear and certain again. But, if examined closely, his claim was strange indeed. He couldn't remember what he had done, but could clearly remember what he *hadn't* done. He couldn't recall abusing the girls, but could recall that no attempt at intercourse was made during the abuse.

Arrested after that incident, Garrow was held on several very serious charges. He had dodged a bullet six weeks earlier when the student kidnapping charges were dismissed, but his future now looked bleak indeed. With eight years already served in prison for rape, it seemed likely Robert would be confined to jail until his court appearance, and would eventually be put away for a long, long time.

However, Armani managed to obtain his release on bail, which the judge inexplicably set at $2,500, a minimal sum considering the gravity of the charges. Arraignment was scheduled for July 12, but in the interim, Robert would have to appear before his parole officer. The results of that meeting could send him to jail, and eventually back to prison.

But, in spite of Garrow's previous criminal record, the parole officer decided there was "no probable cause" that he had committed the crimes, and that revocation was unnecessary. He would remain free until his next scheduled court appearance.

Though he had escaped incarceration so far in both the student kidnapping incident and the Geddes abduction, Robert was more agitated than ever. Great pressures once again began to build from all the stress. He was working six days a week, with shifts ranging from twelve to twenty hours, and he knew the parole officer wanted to take away his driver's license until the pending charges had been settled.

Gripped with fear and dread that his arrest was imminent, Garrow was on constant watch for any type of law officer. All of those things pressed on him until he felt he had to escape. "Escape," as he described it, was to commit rapes and assaults. And a rare form of selective amnesia conveniently erased the memories.

In fact, the only time Robert professed happiness was after returning home from one of his unexplained disappearances. "When I'd come home, I'd be full of smiles and everything. In fact, I had just wanted to get away."

[While Garrow was recounting several serious crimes, the following incident was overlooked, and appeared in later testimony. Portions of the story are placed here to maintain the chronological sequence of events.—Editor.]

As the pressures of the pending Geddes case mounted, Robert once again pulled a disappearing act. Attorney Belge asked him for the details, and Garrow held nothing back.

"Let's see, there was another one after that. I don't know what the day was or whenever it was, but that is the day, and there was another young lady involved. In other words, to put it bluntly, she is dead. I don't know what day, honest. I know it had to be in July, sometime. Last year, '73. That was probably part of the reason I was scared, running."

The courtroom froze. Garrow quickly dodged responsibility for the crime, claiming he had reconstructed the story from pieces given to him by detectives during questioning, and from information provided by his own attorneys.

Robert described the events of that day succinctly. He took his son to school, and then stopped at a restaurant for breakfast. The next thing he knew, he was at home, all smiles, asking his wife if she'd like to go grocery shopping.

Then, with Francis Belge leading the way, Garrow began to tell the story he had "pieced together" over the months, about a young female hitchhiker he had picked up that morning. "She told me she was hitchhiking and skipping school. I drove the car up to where all the apartment houses are now in back of Hughes [Elementary School], and pulled into the driveway that goes in to the apartments, and got out of the car. I know we had a blanket, a brown blanket.

"We got out of the car, we walked all the way down East Colvin, as far as the railroad, and then we crossed over. We went up a hill, and we went into the woods. We both walked together, I had her hand in my hand, so, you know."

He took the girl into a wooded area of Oakwood Cemetery, a section of the eighty-two acre tract that had not yet been developed. Garrow continued, "It's right across the street from where I live. What took place? We had intercourse. Well, she took her clothes off, because I asked her to, and she took them off, there was no fights, no arguments, no nothing. Did she completely disrobe? Yes, everything. In fact, she asked me if I wanted her to take everything off, if that'll help you any, and I says 'Yes.' Then we had intercourse."

To this point, the tale sounded as if Garrow was describing a couple of teenagers on a date. The effect on listeners was one of creepiness and revulsion. Perhaps he was insane after all.

"After, she started putting her clothes on, and we started walking up the hill, and she finished dressing. We went up a little further, and I wanted to have sexual intercourse again, and I don't know, everything just ... all I can do is surmise, is by saying that we were getting deeper in the woods, and I guess maybe she got scared or something, I don't know what, but the point is, we got tangled up, we got to fighting, and I had a knife with me, and she grabbed for it, and I think ... I don't know if I had a rope or a wire. I picked it up ... but anyways, I strangled her, or she was strangled. I don't know if I did it, but she was strangled, let's say. I'm not sure. I think I did, but I'm not sure.

"I don't know how old she was. I don't know. She could have been sixteen, seventeen, eighteen, I don't know. I don't even know her name. I was told her name, and pictures were shown, Frank showed me her picture. I don't remember her name, I don't know."

After killing the girl, he left the cemetery and began to walk, first towards downtown, and then on several other streets before returning to where the car was parked. When he arrived home, according to Garrow, "My wife asked me where I had been, and I said 'I don't know.' She said I was happy as can be, you know what I mean."

The date of that incident, when he raped and killed the young girl, was July 11, 1973. Significantly, it was the day before his scheduled appearance in court for the abduction and assault of the two Geddes girls.

For nearly a year now, Syracuse authorities had made Garrow their prime suspect in the disappearance of sixteen-year-old Alicia Hauck. There was no longer a need for suspicion. Garrow had just admitted to her rape and murder. Every person in the courtroom was gripped with shock, amazement, and dismay at what they were hearing.

Still, Robert Garrow had more to tell, and with Belge nudging him onward, he did so.

Later, on the same day that he killed the girl in the cemetery, Robert visited his parole officer. Ironically, he became upset when the officer accused him of "going around to schools and picking up young girls." Garrow denied it, just hours after he had raped and strangled a local teenager.

The officer asked for his driver's license, but Robert was allowed to keep it for the time being because his family was waiting in the car, and he had groceries to bring home. The license wasn't actually turned in until twelve days later. Much would happen in the interim.

Garrow made another stop that day, at a Sears & Roebuck store, where he purchased a Winchester lever-action rifle. On the following day, apparently still feeling pressure, he skipped his scheduled court appearance on the Geddes charges and left the city, driving north. Robert testified he was on his way to bring a cane to Mineville for his father, who had recently suffered a heart attack.

Considering the terrible past they shared, it is hard to imagine why Garrow would be bringing his father a cane, or anything else that might be considered helpful. Then again, on his left arm, Robert inexplicably sported a heart-shaped tattoo emblazoned with "Mom and Dad." After years of beatings, and once planning to kill his parents, what perverse reasoning could explain that?

At any rate, instead of appearing in court on the Geddes charges, Garrow vanished from sight for several days. He claimed to be hiding out at home for part of that time, but no one knows for certain. He made at least one false start for Mineville, but returned home. Since his memory of those few days was so foggy, it may have indicated he was busy committing other serious crimes.

Then, without telling anyone, he headed north for the Adirondack Mountains on Saturday, July 14. It's about a four-hour drive from Syracuse to Mineville, and Robert wasn't feeling well on the trip. After about three hours, a powerful headache induced him to pull off the main highway onto a dirt road, where he lay over the steering wheel and slept.

When he finally awakened, it was to the sound of a car horn. A glance in the mirror revealed the source, a vehicle stopped in the road directly behind him. Robert's car was parked where the path narrowed, blocking access to the woods road.

Garrow told a hushed courtroom what happened next. "This guy come up to the door, and he had long hair. I must have said something to him, I don't know what, but also during all this time I had my rifles and stuff, camping equipment, I want you to know that.

"I don't know what I said to him, but I said something, because he got mad. He opened my car door, and I slipped out, and we got in an argument and a big scuffle over it. Before I knew it we were down over the embankment, and of course ... of course, I'm putting pieces together again, you know, because I don't know exactly what happened.

"I can't tell exactly, but I try to tell you as much as I can by putting the pieces together. This guy got killed, by a knife, and I was told he was stabbed several times, he was cut across the chest. And I also was told they found him next to a tree, but he wasn't tied, I don't think they said."

He added later, "I know the place, Wevertown, that's it, in Wevertown, where it happened. I don't remember stabbing him. She [the girlfriend] came out to help him, and I hit her."

At that point in his testimony, Garrow rambled on at length about later "piecing the story together," and then mentioned the ride north in the ambulance after his capture in Witherbee. During that trip, he had been asked about the murder at Wevertown, and said he was beaten after claiming to have no memory of the incident.

"If I knew it beforehand, I would have told the BCIs when they worked me over and kicked me between the legs and everything. I would have told them everything, just to get rid of them. I would have signed statements and everything. Did you ever get kicked between the legs? I did, half a dozen times."

The killing that Garrow had just described was that of

Daniel Porter. Dread filled the courtroom as everyone present anticipated what was coming next. Susan Petz was already known to be dead, and now they would hear the grisly details of her final days.

Garrow went on to tell how he took Petz north to near his childhood home on Barton Hill at Witherbee. He described a pleasant drive, and as she helped him unload the car, "she was very polite and everything. We had a wonderful conversation." He made it all sound like a delightful summer outing.

Garrow said they engaged in intercourse and various other sexual acts several times over the next three days. On Monday, July 16, her third day of captivity, is when Garrow said Susan Petz made a last, desperate attempt to escape.

They had retrieved water from the area of several mineshafts, part of Robert's plan for them to bathe. When she refused his order to remove her blouse, an argument ensued. Upset, Garrow laid his knife and rifle on the ground while he removed his shirt.

The mineshafts were located at the bottom of the small mountain, not far from a road. Sensing a possibility for escape, Susan grabbed the knife. Garrow reacted quickly, snatching it from her, but badly cutting his hand in the process.

He then stabbed her and disposed of her body down a mineshaft vent. When he described how he got rid of the body, Belge asked, "Was that the one I found?" Garrow answered, "Yes."

It seemed an innocuous exchange at the time, but would prove to be of tremendous importance later, setting off a sequence of events that sparked an intense national debate.

After killing Petz, Garrow made his way through the woods to near the Belfry Tower Road, and then went to the home of his sister, Agnes Mandy. To explain his torn shirt and bloodied hand, he told her he was camping on Barton Hill, and had slipped and cut himself on some glass.

Agnes treated his injury, and at his behest, she called Edith, who said Frank Armani wanted him to return home as soon as possible. Garrow claimed Armani wanted his help with some chores, but it is far more likely he was concerned that Robert had missed his July 12 court appearance without explanation.

At around 11:00 p.m., Robert retrieved his car from its hiding place on Belfry Tower Road, and returned to Syracuse by around 4:00 a.m. on Tuesday, July 17.

After spending Tuesday in Syracuse, Garrow and his entire family were waiting in Agnes' driveway in Witherbee when she woke up on Wednesday morning. That night, the two Garrow children slept at Agnes Mandy's house, while Robert and Edith camped together on Barton Hill, where he had just held Susan Petz captive for three days before killing her.

On the next day, Garrow took his son, Robert, Jr., to the same campsite, where they spent the night. On Friday, July 20, the family returned to Syracuse. It was also on July 20 that Daniel Porter's body was discovered near Wevertown, and the frantic search for Susan Petz began.

For the next several days, Robert was in virtual hiding, watching fearfully from his home for any sign of police coming to pick him up. He had missed his court appearance on July 12, and the makeup date, July 26, was closing in.

Finally, the day arrived. He rose early, around 6:00 a.m., while Edith was still sleeping. Instead of preparing for his rescheduled arraignment on charges in the Geddes incident, Garrow once again headed north into the mountains.

After more than two hours of driving, he arrived at Speculator, on the shores of Lake Pleasant. Driving around the village, he scouted the different sites, showing particular interest in Camp of the Woods, a Christian family resort. There were plenty of young girls at the camp, perfect prey for Garrow. It nearly proved catastrophic for three of them.

On Friday night, he accosted a young woman, claiming he was a detective. As he attempted to grab her, she broke away and made it safely to the camp building where she was staying.

The next morning he was back again, this time obstructing the path of two young girls on bicycles. Garrow was carrying his rifle, and told the girls he needed a bicycle to go after some gas for his car. They managed to avoid him and wisely rode away, even as Robert threatened them with his firearm.

That night, he parked the car in a roadside rest area just

east of the village and slept in the vehicle.

On Sunday morning, Garrow filled the car with gas, and purchased donuts and coffee for breakfast. Leaving Speculator, he drove a few miles south on Routes 8 and 30 (east of the village), and pulled off on a side road to eat.

As he left the main highway and drove north on Old Route 8, Robert spied a tent by the roadside. Inside were David Freeman and Carol Malinowski.

Though it received only passing mention in court, Garrow apparently considered the situation carefully before actually approaching the tent. After breakfast at Northville, Nick Fiorillo and Phil Domblewski were back at the tent site briefly, and then went fishing for nearly an hour.

When Garrow made his move, there was only one tent standing, and only one car at the site. Yet, he had told Freeman and Malinowski to hurry, "before your friends come back." He could not have known there had been other people at the site unless he had observed them an hour earlier.

And, during his initial contact with the campers, Garrow was wearing a pair of binoculars around his neck. He likely used them to monitor the situation before moving in.

His approach of the single tent, then, was a calculated move, with the intent to rape, and possibly kill. He even had time to scout the woods for a suitable place to tie up his captives, and some of his later comments to the foursome suggested he had done just that. But the delay caused by scouting allowed just enough time for the two fishing companions to return before Garrow could make off with Freeman and Malinowski.

His testimony recounted the abduction of the four campers, and the tying of each of them to trees in the woods. When he described Domblewski's death, Robert's portrayal differed from the story told by the three survivors.

Garrow claimed that he laid both the knife and the gun on the ground, and had nothing but rope in his hands when he faced Domblewski. However, the need for rope was questionable, as Domblewski had been the first one tied to a tree, according to his three companions.

Garrow claimed Domblewski then made a grab for him, and

testified, "I hit him with the knife. As they said, there was no sign of wrestling or anything on the ground, but we did wrestle. After I hit him with the knife, I tied him up to the tree. I remember doing that, and something keeps telling me in my mind that I also cut the rope after, but I am not sure on that."

For some reason, the prosecution paid little attention to the similarities described by Robert in all four murders. A close comparison suggests the stories were contrived unimaginatively by Garrow, and, in fact, were almost identical tales.

Porter struggled over the knife, while Hauck, Petz, and Domblewski all were stabbed after lunging for it. There was one common denominator: Garrow was the only surviving witness to all four murders.

The stories were told just as he wished them to be told, and in Garrow's version of events, he was under attack in each fatal confrontation. His accounts suggested it was the fault of the victims for moving against him, but the marks on some of their bodies betrayed Garrow's stories of self-defense.

None of them showed signs of having been slain by a sudden assault. Multiple minor cuts and scratches in addition to large, deep wounds suggested calculated, deliberate stabbings. Undeniably, some of his victims died slowly, tormented until the final blows were delivered by a cold-blooded killer.

The surviving campers knew that Garrow was lying. They had all observed Domblewski being the first tied to a tree, and he was found later in the same position, deceased. Malinowski saw him before she fled, and Fiorillo led troopers to the site later.

Domblewski's arms were still behind him around the tree, though the rope was missing. Photographic evidence offered to the jury confirmed their stories. Daniel Porter had been found in much the same fashion.

With acknowledgment of the attack described by the three surviving campers, Robert's most recent crime had been revealed. There may have been many other previous victims, but Domblewski was the last. And this dangerous criminal, now an admitted serial rapist and serial killer, sought to insulate himself from blame behind claims of periodic memory blackouts.

Garrow's claims of intermittent recollections were dealt

a severe blow under cross-examination by prosecutor Norman Mordue. During Robert's final moments on the stand, Mordue backtracked through earlier events, questioning him at length on the gruesome story of the bull's slaughter.

It seemed as if Mordue was simply clarifying a few points made during earlier testimony, and Robert readily answered the questions. But Mordue was laying the groundwork for a sardonic, scathing final assessment of Garrow's memory problems.

After eliciting several seemingly insignificant details of the event from Garrow, Mordue completed the setup by delivering one of the most memorable lines of the entire trial: "Now, you can recall back to then, of killing the bull, trying to use heavy shells, six shots in the chamber, the type of weapon, using the twenty-pound sledge, and who was there. But you can't recall what you did with Philip Domblewski, can you?"

Belge's objection was quickly sustained by Marthen, but Mordue had made his point, and ended with "Judge, I have nothing further."

It was undeniably a stellar moment for the prosecution.

During other testimony, including extensive cross-examinations, Garrow revealed a few details of the lengthy manhunt near Speculator. He confirmed that he was frequently within sight of searchers, staying close to the road, but taking full advantage of the thick forest cover to remain hidden. When bloodhounds pursued him, he crossed and re-crossed streams, attempting to disperse his scent.

At one point, near the state police command post along Route 8, Garrow was moving across an open area under cover of darkness when he struck his head on part of a helicopter. Robert claimed he considered stealing it, since he was familiar with helicopters, having worked on them during his stint in the military. He thought better of trying to take it because modern helicopters were fuel-injected and needed about twelve minutes to warm up before takeoff.

Though he may have had some knowledge of helicopters from his time in the military, it strained credulity to suggest that Garrow might have been capable of stealing and piloting one. He began in the service as an MP, and spent most of his eighteen months imprisoned, leaving precious little time for training on such a complex piece of equipment.

Among Robert's other recollections during testimony was an encounter with a snake. As he told the courtroom, "I grabbed hold of the snake, and I remember eating the snake because I was so hungry and because I had no food to eat ... I don't know what kind it was. I was just hungry. I remember eating, and spitting something out, I don't know what ... bones or what ... but I know one thing. At the time, it must have been very delicious to me, because when you're hungry, you're hungry, and you eat anything, because I couldn't get no berries. I couldn't see 'em. I had no glasses."

The snake story evoked revulsion, but it paled in comparison to the effect of listening for three days to Garrow's brutal life story and his barbaric crimes. The experience left trial attendees shell-shocked.

Newspapers throughout New York and across the nation carried the grisly story beneath blaring headlines. Garrow's terrible confessions made for gripping news coverage in all media. Four murders and seven rapes—and all revealed by the defense! The bombshell effect cannot be overstated.

As the trial continued, Garrow's memory and his mental condition became the prime focus of attention. Though some psychiatrists believed his stories of occasional memory loss, others were far from convinced.

Mordue asked Dr. William Holt if he was able to reach any deductions regarding Garrow's amnesia, prompting this memorable exchange:

Holt: "I came to the conclusion that since the most obvious segment of time forgotten, allegedly forgotten, by the subject was exactly the time in which the crime was committed, that this was a self-serving effort to avoid disclosure of what had transpired."

Mordue: "Is that sort of amnesia given a name?"

Holt: "I would call it lying."

Regarding Garrow's cooperation during their sessions, Holt said, "It fluctuated. On questions that did not pertain to difficulty with the law, he generally cooperated. In fact, he volunteered accounts of his life experiences as a boy on a farm, also as to his studying in prison, and as to the importance of his present job."

When asked about elements of the stories regarding crime, said Holt, "He repeatedly replied that he did not remember."

Dr. Walter Osinski came to a similar determination. Said Osinski, "We felt that there was inconsistency in his alleged memory deficits, that he didn't have the typical kind of amnesia that psychotic individuals or people with organic brain disease have; that, in fact, the kind of alleged memory impairment that he showed was more like that we see in individuals who are trying to avoid telling the truth."

Several psychiatrists and psychologists offered professional opinions on Garrow's erratic behavior. Their comments were based largely on extensive testing performed at multiple facilities. Included were I.Q. tests, inkblot tests, a neurological examination, an electroencephalogram, a brain scan, and a variety of intelligence and behavioral tests.

The doctors also listened to hours of tape recordings of Garrow's conversations with his lawyers, and interviews with Agnes and Florence. Some reviewed Garrow's own testimony and the testimony of the three surviving campers.

There was talk of thought disorder, psychosis, sociopathic personality, immaturity, antisocial personality, pathological sexuality, mental deficiency, split personality, brain disease, psychopathic behavior, personality disorders, amnesia, and schizophrenia.

During the mental examinations, Garrow at times seemed to be toying with the psychiatrists, recalling certain details for defense doctors, but claiming some type of amnesia for their prosecution counterparts.

Role-playing was employed by one pair of psychiatrists, eliciting displays by Garrow that were described in court as frightening. At one point, Dr. Jerry Morrow, who conducted the role-playing sessions, characterized him as "terrifyingly sadistic."

Among the various symptoms ascribed to Garrow were hallucinations, affectation by magnetic forces, voices whispering in his ears, a roaring sound in his ears, electronic sounds, music from outer space, restlessness, and the inability to fantasize.

As expected, the findings often took opposing positions. Some deduced that Garrow was insane, and therefore not responsible for the crimes he had committed, since a mental defect or disease was at fault. Others claimed the exact opposite.

Many found his stories highly unlikely, and his spotty memory nothing more than a convenience. Everyone agreed there was lying going on to some degree. It all seemed geared towards confirming Robert's insanity plea. In effect, he would be guilty, but not responsible.

Some expressed the suspicion that he was a proficient actor. To that effect, it was noted that strange forces seem to take control of him during his crimes, and he often appeared troubled and anti-social. Yet those same doctors were admittedly puzzled that Garrow was clearly garrulous and social during court recesses, sharing stories with deputies and reporters.

Besides the professional witnesses, a number of others took the stand, including Robert's sisters and his mother. Margaret Garrow's performance was a sad, frustrating, and ultimately failed effort at communication. Despite several decades living in Mineville, she still spoke barely intelligible English, and often didn't seem to understand the questions that were posed.

Offering nothing positive on Robert's behalf, she became more of a visual display for the defense, providing a look at Robert's roots, and suggesting he might not be entirely at fault for his problems. Belge would say that and more in his closing arguments.

As the trial progressed, a separate but critical issue developed, soon taking on a life of its own. It began on day two of Robert's testimony, and involved an exchange of only seven words. Millions of words would be written about that exchange in the coming years.

The great controversy developed with the revelation that Garrow's attorneys had previous knowledge of other homicides their client had committed. Day by day, the ripple effect of that disclosure grew, and soon Armani and Belge faced a tsunami of criticism.

From brief comments during testimony, information was

developed indicating that both attorneys knew the locations of the Petz and Hauck bodies months in advance of authorities. For many, this was as shocking and disgusting as some of Garrow's own personal history.

Armani and Belge had kept the information to themselves, even as hundreds searched desperately for the two girls and the families suffered through an agonizing wait. The lawyers were vilified in the media and had few defenders. They claimed the sanctity of the attorney-client privilege, but officials were outraged, and the public was horrified.

With the maelstrom of accusations and the specter of legal charges looming against them, Armani and Belge were besieged from all sides, while still trying to conduct their defense of Garrow. When an official complaint was made to the New York State Bar Association by William Hauck, Alicia's father, it was announced that the two attorneys would be investigated for misconduct.

By this time the trial was winding down. Armani and Belge trained their attention on Garrow's case, avoiding the distraction of their own pending legal troubles. There would be plenty of time later to defend their conduct.

After ten days of sometimes riveting, and often frightening, testimony, both sides presented their final summations on June 27. The defense argued that the jury should be prepared to consider a lesser charge, possibly first-degree manslaughter under severe emotional distress.

In his closing statement, Belge said it was Robert Garrow's parents who should have been on trial, and he asked for a verdict of not guilty by reason of insanity, emphasizing that "we have admitted to four murders and seven rapes."

Belge's impassioned plea on behalf of his client was acknowledged by opponent Norman Mordue, who commented, "I was personally concerned that sympathy could enter into the jury's deliberations after listening to Mr. Belge." It was a professional nod to a worthy, skilled opponent.

In spite of the effective defense summation, after only two hours, the jury returned a verdict of guilty. Belge immediately gave notice the defense would file an appeal based on the rejection of the change of venue request, and the fact that Garrow was not tried by a jury of his peers, since the average age of the jury was over sixty-two years old.

Onondaga County D.A. Holcombe praised the efforts of his assistant, Norman Mordue, who had joined Intemann in the prosecution effort. He also indicated that a timetable was forthcoming on the prosecution of Garrow in Onondaga County, and that legal action was being prepared against Armani and Belge for not disclosing the whereabouts of Alicia Hauck's body once they became privy to that information.

Judge Marthen set a sentencing date of July 8 for Garrow. But, in a surprise move, the judge delivered the sentence a week early at the request of Garrow's attorneys. On July 1, Hamilton County's first convicted murderer in nearly half a century was sentenced to a term of twenty-five years to life.

When asked by the judge if he had any comment, Garrow said in a very soft voice, "Just that I'm sorry."

On the very next day, the defendant was taken to Clinton Correctional Facility in Dannemora. Once again, Robert Garrow was going home.

8

Ethics: The Legal Profession Shaken to its Core

When he was first captured in August 1973, Garrow spent nearly six weeks in the hospital while his wounds healed. He remained tight-lipped there in the presence of law enforcement officials, but with his attorneys, Frank Armani and Francis Belge, it was a different story.

Garrow trusted Armani, who had been his personal attorney for some time and had helped get him out of trouble more than once in the past. To handle the murder charges, Armani had enlisted the aid of Belge, an outstanding trial lawyer. Garrow soon realized he would have to trust them equally.

When the two attorneys first interviewed Garrow in anticipation of preparing a defense strategy, they urged him to tell the complete truth. Both men got far more than they bargained for.

Garrow gave them details on what had happened with Philip Domblewski, but then began to talk about other crimes, including three additional homicides. Of the three, two involved missing persons who remained the focus of law enforcement search teams.

Armani and Belge later said they didn't know whether to believe their client at the time. He might have just been some attention-seeking whacko, laying claim to crimes he had read about or was questioned about. It was not an unheard of occurrence in the world of criminal law.

The two attorneys pressed him for details, and Garrow drew maps guiding them to each body. He described the location of one girl in the old iron mines at Witherbee near his childhood home. The other girl was said to be in a cemetery across the road from where Garrow lived in Syracuse.

At that point, it seemed likely the two skilled attorneys could link those locations to the disappearances of Susan Petz in the Adirondacks and Alicia Hauck in Syracuse, and safely assume their client was being truthful. After all, they possessed information far beyond what the police new, and authorities had long considered Garrow the prime suspect in both crimes.

Still, Armani and Belge felt compelled to actually visit the sites mapped out by Garrow. By locating both corpses, they would eliminate concerns that he somehow might have concocted the stories.

In late August, shortly after Garrow's capture, they used his hand-drawn map of the Witherbee location and followed his instructions, but to no avail. According to Belge, it took five trips to the site before they met with success. They passed close by the mineshaft many times before finally locating it at dusk one evening, using a flashlight.

Armani held Belge's legs tightly and lowered him into the opening so he could see Petz's body, which was naked from the waist up. Belge snapped some photos to record the find.

Next, they turned their attention towards locating the Hauck girl in Syracuse. Garrow provided a general diagram of the area, and Belge found the body around the end of September, using a method of squaring off the area with markers. But there was more to the story that he wasn't telling just yet. Details would emerge later.

At the time, both men believed the discovery of other crime victims fell under the attorney-client privilege. They only found the bodies because Garrow had given them directions, and unless he authorized them to release the information, they were bound to secrecy.

There existed one exception to that circumstance: if releasing the information would prevent a crime from being committed, they were required to speak out. With Garrow in custody, injured, unable to walk, and heavily guarded, that seemed highly unlikely. Since there was no threat of additional crimes, the information remained confidential.

Nine months later, during the second day of Garrow's testimony, he revealed the location of the bodies, releasing both attorneys from the vow of secrecy. After the day's court proceedings ended, the judge entertained motions.

Norman Mordue requested the drawings, maps, and photographs produced during Armani and Belge's efforts to find the bodies. Belge said they wanted to tell the parents what they had found, but client confidentiality forced them to destroy the materials, including the photo negatives.

Mordue asked if they could at least know when the photographs were taken. The testy reply from Belge: "It was the same time that the state police were following us with a helicopter and a couple of airplanes, whatever dates those were." With that, the stage was set for future legal fireworks.

Belge was sarcastically referring to a law-enforcement detail secretly assigned to track the two attorneys. Apparently it hadn't been so secret after all.

Later that day Armani and Belge spoke with the media, explaining how they had found both bodies, and how difficult it had been to remain silent.

Their comments at the news conference reflected the angst both men had suffered during the intervening months until the victims were finally discovered by others. Said Belge, "We both, knowing how the parents must feel, wanted to advise the parents where the bodies were. I spent many, many sleepless nights over the inability to reveal the information, especially after Mr. Petz came in from Chicago and talked to me."

Armani said much the same in reference to William Hauck's daughter, adding, "Death is difficult to accept. It's difficult enough, but worrying and wondering, it'll drive you insane."

When those statements were made by Armani and Belge, the trial was still in its early stages, and Garrow's own sensational testimony was grabbing headlines everywhere. The attorney controversy received voluminous publicity, but, at least temporarily, it was relegated to the sidelines, giving way to the daily shocking revelations by Garrow.

As comments began to appear in the media, decrying the attorneys' behavior, their courtroom opponents jumped on the bandwagon, playing to the criticisms expressed far and wide. However, prosecutors likely had some inkling that the issue was far more complicated than was being portrayed in the media.

As newspaper editorials and letters to the editor fairly screamed for action against the attorneys, others began to weigh in on the issue. Jon Holcombe was not directly involved in the Garrow trial, but the Alicia Hauck case was within his jurisdiction. Holcombe said a decision about prosecuting Armani and Belge would be made once the Garrow trial had ended.

At the same time, the parents of Susan Petz expressed shock, dismay, and anger at the lawyers' actions. William Hauck spoke out in a similar manner.

In early September 1973, Hauck had publicly expressed hope that his daughter would be found alive, and offered a reward of $1,000 for information on her whereabouts. His anxiety and pain could have ended shortly after, when the two attorney's found his daughter's body in late September.

Instead, he was forced to live the nightmare for another nine weeks, until she was finally recovered by authorities in early December. The public was outraged.

Further exploiting the situation during the trial, and certainly increasing the vitriol directed at Armani and Belge, prosecutor William Intemann made another shocking disclosure. Not only had the two attorneys withheld the information about the location of the bodies, but they had used that knowledge in seeking a plea bargain for Garrow.

Normally, the particulars of such conferences were kept confidential. The revelation by Intemann effectively threw gasoline on the flames of controversy. It was just three days later that William Hauck filed his complaint, followed shortly by the launch of an official investigation into the lawyers' conduct.

The police were ordered to conduct a preliminary inquiry, and after examining the evidence, it was concluded that the lawyers had acted lawfully. In spite of that finding, Holcombe's office continued to pursue the case.

Further complicating matters for Armani and Belge were attacks on several other fronts. The families of Petz and Hauck announced they were considering filing civil lawsuits against the attorneys, even as the Garrow trial continued. Assistant D.A. Emil Rossi told reporters he was looking into the public health law and the statute that governed evidence tampering, both of which may have been violated by Garrow's attorneys.

By trial's end, the attorney-client privilege issue was being debated across the nation. Armani and Belge had become the center of attention, most of it bad, and some of it dangerous, including death threats. Public scorn focused on the two men, perceived now as villains nearly as evil as Garrow himself.

Many in the legal profession began to realize the magnitude of the case evolving from the actions of Garrow's attorneys. Much was at stake here, going right to the very core of the legal system. The outcome of the attack on Robert Garrow's attorneys would have a bearing on the actions of every lawyer within the nation's borders, and perhaps beyond.

In the simplest of terms, if a client couldn't speak to an attorney without fear of reprisal, then the attorney would not be able to provide the best defense possible. One of the basic tenets of the United States justice system was suddenly in the spotlight. Public scrutiny of such an emotional subject caused many lawyers to squirm uncomfortably.

As the importance of the issue became apparent, rhetoric was discouraged. Legal experts referred to the case as unprecedented, and Onondaga County officials felt the decision was far too complex and important for a lower court to settle. This was a matter for the highest level of jurists in the state, the Court of Appeals.

Public debate continued, but legal officials were forced to remain silent. State law required total secrecy for investigations of such a sensitive nature. While the inquiry was announced during Garrow's trial, state judiciary officials delayed action until the trial's conclusion to ensure their findings would not affect its outcome.

The high court didn't waste any time honoring its promise to examine the case. On the last day of the trial, it was announced that the appellate court had directed the New York State Bar Association's Committee on Lawyer Responsibility to begin investigating the actions of the two lawyers.

The case against the attorneys also had political ramifications for those who held various offices, and those who sought to unseat the incumbents. Posturing began at a very high level as party leaders began jockeying for position.

Robert Meehan, chairman of the board of New York State district attorneys, and Democratic candidate for state attorney general, was highly critical of Armani and Belge, calling their behavior "appalling." He added, "Justice and morality were not given first priority."

In early July 1974, just days after Garrow's trial ended, Holcombe again jumped into the fray, issuing an extensive statement denouncing the attorneys' behavior. The next day he confirmed that both lawyers would be pursued for multiple violations and unethical behavior.

Whether or not his argument was rock solid, Holcombe was trying the case in the court of public opinion, and the deck was stacked heavily in his favor. He cited research findings portraying the attorney-client privilege as limited, and said it may not have even existed in the Garrow case. A few days later, he announced that Onondaga County's grand jury would be considering criminal charges against Armani and Belge.

Bolstering Holcombe's public efforts were dozens of letters appearing in the principal Syracuse newspapers. In one day alone, contributors used the terms appalled, disgusted, horrified, sick, fury, revulsion, and abhorrence in reference to Armani and Belge's behavior. Until then, those words had been reserved solely for their infamous client.

Holcombe came out with an eight-page statement detailing the perceived wrongs committed by Armani and Belge, plus a five-page letter to Police Chief Thomas Sardino, reviewing the D.A.'s plans for pursuit of the charges. Both documents were released to the media.

In the statement, Holcombe said the attorneys had disturbed a crime scene when they illegally moved a body to photograph it. By leaving the Hauck remains in the cemetery, they had also violated state law providing the right to a decent burial. Thus, the facts of the case mandated review by a grand jury.

He also claimed they used secret information on the location of the bodies to gain a tactical advantage during a plea-bargain session. Holcombe characterized the attempt as "monstrous," and further charged that, when the lawyers destroyed photographs and maps, they had illegally destroyed evidence.

In closing, he added that the lawyers' actions had cost the taxpayers dearly. New York State police had expended an extra 35,000 hours of duty that could have been avoided, and Syracuse police had used 350 additional hours.

In denying he had moved a body, Armani said, "The statement is untrue." He also pointed out the case had already been referred to the state appellate court. As a public official, it was improper for Holcombe to be commenting before the investigation was completed. Taking it a step further, Armani suggested he might file a grievance against the D.A.

Belge, on the other hand, was nowhere to be found. It was suspected that he was the main target of Holcombe's efforts. On previous occasions, the two of them had engaged in fiery debate. More was sure to come.

Though public opinion was solidly on the side of Holcombe, the opposite was true among legal experts. The nationwide debate spawned many commentaries and reports supporting the attorneys' behavior. In general, it was believed by highly placed legal scholars that Armani and Belge had indeed behaved ethically.

Several law school deans had taken that stance, but there were still many attorneys who felt the two men were wrong morally, ethically, and professionally. Of course, none of them had ever been in Armani and Belge's situation. Amidst the raging controversy, Armani said little, and Belge said nothing.

That was about to change. Frank Armani was preparing to go before the Onondaga County grand jury, but he would not be going alone. Manhattan criminal defense attorney Elliot A. Taikeff had offered free legal services to Armani. Like many litigators across the state, the New York City lawyer realized how critical the outcome would be. This was a test case with huge implications.

Taikeff came out firing on behalf of his client. Citing the plea-bargain session held in September 1973, he argued that the D.A.'s actions were disingenuous and self-serving. If Holcombe felt the two men were subject to charges based on what occurred in that session, then he should have taken immediate action to bring them before a grand jury.

Instead, he had waited ten months to do so. It was noted from other sources that the move by Holcombe was politically expedient, as he was in the midst of a re-election campaign. Attaching himself to a high-profile, popular cause was an excellent way to attract voters' attention.

Within two weeks, Taikeff filed two motions on behalf of Armani, one of them a highly unusual move. Taikeff argued before the court for the right to challenge any grand jury member who might be biased in their judgment, having been exposed to unrelenting negative publicity against his client.

The second part of Taikeff's motion requested that a supreme court justice give instructions to the grand jury on laws that applied to the case. That is a job normally performed by the district attorney, in this instance Jon Holcombe.

Taikeff's move suggested that Holcombe had been so outspoken against Armani and Belge, he may be disinclined to do the thorough job necessary ensuring that the grand jurists were appropriately charged.

Said Taikeff, "Publicity in the case has not only been massive and intense, it has been generally unfavorable to Armani, as has been the reaction of the public to a complex, little-understood area of professional responsibility."

Holcombe filed countermotions with the court, and the two sides prepared to do battle in early August. However, Supreme Court Justice Parker Stone sent the case back to Onondaga County. Stone pointed out that grand juries reported to county court judges; therefore, arguments must also be presented before county judges.

The attorneys subsequently appeared before Onondaga County Judge Ormand Gale, who denied Taikeff's request to have the grand jurors examined, but reserved judgment on the motion to have the jurors instructed by a judge instead of the district attorney.

Taikeff had effectively cited several direct quotations of Holcombe, bringing into question his ability to remain impartial in dealing with the jurors. Included by Taikeff was the D.A.'s letter to the police chief, which said, in part, "The most terrifying of all was the continued emotional wrong done to the parents, relatives, and friends of the unburied. No law should sanction such conduct."

Meanwhile, Francis Belge returned to court and received authorization from Judge Gale to continue with Armani as one of Garrow's court-appointed attorneys. Despite Holcombe's pursuit of charges against the two attorneys, Belge said he wasn't concerned about the D.A. His top priority was defending his client.

Both Armani and Belge remained tight-lipped regarding the investigation into their conduct, but several prominent attorneys spoke out on their behalf. Holcombe, on the other hand, was anything but reticent, issuing statements even when no new information was forthcoming. He seemed almost obsessive in his zeal, pursuing the case publicly and attacking from all angles.

One segment of the law addressing client-confidentiality states that a lawyer must release information if it would prevent a crime from being committed. In a convoluted bit of reasoning, Holcombe claimed that not reporting a body to authorities violated the Public Health Law, and in effect, was an ongoing crime itself. Therefore, the two lawyers were required to reveal the information as soon as they possessed it.

It was twisted logic, and a less than convincing argument.

The case against Garrow's attorneys again influenced the upcoming political campaign. Holcombe was hit by several broadsides from the Democratic candidate for district attorney, Melvin Slotnick, who accused him of grandstanding. Said Slotnick, "Finally, the D.A. states that he does not wish to discuss the Garrow case, even though he was the one who initiated much of the publicity on it."

Slotnick also attacked Holcombe for public posturing, and using the case for his personal advantage. "This has become a political issue in Holcombe's hands. He waited until just before the election this year to schedule a grand jury investigation ... this is a typical example of Mr. Holcombe in his passion to obtain pre-trial publicity."

Echoing Taikeff's claim, the Democratic challenger noted

that it was Holcombe who caused the Petz and Hauck families to suffer by not asking for an immediate grand jury investigation in September 1973. Slotnick added that he wouldn't pursue the point any further, as the county bar association had asked him to avoid making the Garrow and Armani case a major campaign issue.

In mid-September 1974, Judge Ormand Gale announced he had granted Elliot Taikeff's motion to have the court provide instructions to the grand jurors, a task normally handled by the district attorney. The decision surprised many, but the gravity of the situation was reflected in Taikeff's request, which said, "This case presents complex and sensitive legal questions which go to the very fabric of our constitutional system."

In late November, the grand jury began its investigation into the conduct of Armani and Belge, and also planned to consider charges against Robert Garrow in the murder of Alicia Hauck.

Three months later, in early February 1975, Frank Armani received a subpoena to appear before the Onondaga County grand jury. Armani, taking the high road, waived immunity from prosecution. Said his attorney, Taikeff, on the matter: "If Armani testified and was not indicted, there would always be a question unanswered—was it because he received immunity, or because he did nothing wrong?"

During Armani's testimony, he told how the decision to honor his client's confidence had not been taken lightly. In view of that, he had pursued other counsel, seeking advice from a government official and from "a very high-ranking judge in this state."

According to Taikeff, Armani sought a means of revealing the information to the parents without violating his oath of confidentiality. The government official Armani spoke with had, in turn, referred him to the high-ranking judge. According to Armani, the judge told him, "Under no circumstances could he reveal the information."

The judge who advised Armani had, until that time, remained nameless, but was called to testify before the grand jury. He was later identified as State Supreme Court Justice

Frank Delvecchio.

In short order, the grand jury cleared Armani of any wrongdoing. The jury also requested that the judge forward pertinent testimony to the New York State Bar Association, which was handling the state's investigation of Armani and Belge. Said the relieved Armani, "I believe this vindicates the concept of the attorney-client relationship."

The grand jury did return two sealed indictments, prompting speculation as to the specifics. It was widely believed that one applied to Garrow's prosecution in the Hauck murder. The other was suspected to be an indictment of Francis Belge, which seemed contradictory, since he and Armani had worked together and had been accused of the same offenses.

However, it was rumored that Belge would be charged with violating the Public Health Law. The infraction involved moving the body, or body parts, of Alicia Hauck. Armani had not been present when that occurred.

Jon Holcombe did seem to be paying undue attention to the pursuit of Francis Belge. Slick, experienced, and aggressive, Belge would not make an easy target. And, when backed into a corner, he was prepared to fight his way out.

After the grand jury completed its work, Holcombe was off to the National D.A.'s Convention in Hawaii. Francis Belge was off to a much less exotic location, but was also conducting some important business. Appearing in Hamilton County court, he swore out a complaint against Jon Holcombe, charging him with obstructing governmental justice and official misconduct.

A spokesman for the D.A.'s office said Holcombe had no intention of returning from Hawaii before the convention ended, just to answer the charges. Justice Gene Brooks of the Town of Lake Pleasant signed a warrant for Holcombe's arrest, but William Intemann appeared on behalf of Holcombe, and Brooks withdrew the warrant on grounds of legal insufficiency.

The animosity between Holcombe and Belge was apparent. The charges Belge sought stemmed from an incident that occurred during the Garrow trial, when it was first revealed that Belge and Armani had known the locations of the bodies of Petz and Hauck.

During a recess, Holcombe sharply criticized Belge, allegedly saying, "I'll have your ass if any of the crimes were committed in Onondaga County." Belge characterized it as an attempt to interfere with his defense of Garrow.

Just one day after he filed charges against Holcombe, Belge was arraigned on the two counts in the grand jury indictment, which cited him for preventing a decent burial, and for "importuning another not to report the existence and location of said remains ... and by not himself reporting the existence and location of said remains." Both charges were misdemeanors.

As always, Belge was ready for battle. When read the charges by Judge Gale, he replied, "I believe I am immune from arrest." Belge claimed the Civil Rights Law protected attorneys from arrest if they had an active case before the court. Accordingly, he asked that booking and fingerprinting procedures be suspended.

Belge noted that he did have business before the court. He had been ordered to file briefs in the defense of Robert Garrow in Onondaga County. Judge Gale was forced to reserve judgment, and said he would entertain arguments from Belge and the D.A.'s office on the matter.

Holcombe's office filed court papers claiming Belge was not immune from arrest, and had, in fact, misinterpreted the law. Further complicating matters, the D.A.'s office served notice they might subpoena Armani to testify in Belge's case, even as Armani and Belge were partnered in the defense of Garrow.

Armani commented that, if called, he would certainly testify, and that anything he could contribute to the case would only help Belge.

Garrow may have been convicted and put away, but the media circus that surrounded his trial had hardly abated. Heavy coverage by newspapers, radio, and television had shifted to the ongoing legal battle between the attorneys, and it remained among the high-profile stories of the day, keeping the name Garrow in the public eye.

The D.A. appeared to have his opponent on the ropes, reeling from constant attacks. But Belge counterpunched by filing an affidavit with City Court Judge James Fahey, requesting an arrest warrant for Holcombe on charges of alleged official misconduct, obstructing governmental administration, and tampering with a witness.

In the affidavit, Belge explained that he had enlisted the aid of friend and hunting partner Ralph Kackison to find Alicia Hauck's body. Once Kackison found her, he telephoned Belge, who said words to the effect of, "Oh, my god! He [Garrow] was telling the truth!"

Belge then visited the site and photographed the remains. To do so, he moved the skull, which was detached from the body and lay a short distance away. Before they left the cemetery, Belge made it clear to Kackison that, by law, he also must maintain the confidentiality that Belge was sworn to uphold.

Kackison had attested to those facts before a grand jury in January 1975. After that appearance, he said Holcombe warned him not to talk, saying, "If you do, your life will not be worth a plugged nickel." That statement was included in the affidavit, and was the source of the alleged witness tampering charge.

Belge certainly was a busy man. As he prepared to face off in court against the D.A. to argue his own indictment charges, Holcombe's arrest warrant was still pending. Belge also had a third active case. He and Armani had just been granted an extension by the appellate division of the state supreme court in filing Garrow's appeal of the Domblewski conviction.

March 4, 1975 was not a good day for Francis Belge. Judge Fahey rejected his request for an arrest warrant for Holcombe, saying that city court was not the proper venue for such action. At the same time, Judge Gale denied Belge's claim of immunity from arrest, though he ruled that a criminal procedure law excused the attorney from normal booking procedures.

As Belge worked on Garrow's appeal and planned his own defense against Holcombe, he faced another legal problem unrelated to the Garrow proceedings. It was announced in late March that Belge would stand trial on charges of failure to pay for law books.

A suit filed by Lawyer's Cooperative Publishers said he owed them just under $6,000, and that the bill was already over a year old. They had waited for him to finish with the Garrow trial before seeking a settlement.

Amidst all the legal wrangling, the ethics investigation by the New York State Bar Association was still ongoing. It was believed that any decision would be delayed until final resolution of yet another issue, the pending health law charges.

During his running battle with Belge, Holcombe was also dealt a pair of legal setbacks. The first came from the New York State Supreme Court, but the second was of far greater significance. In dismissing Holcombe's indictment of Francis Belge, Judge Gale said the grand jury was "grasping at straws." He added several statements supporting Belge's conduct.

Rather than take the case before a new grand jury, Holcombe appealed the decision, and just a week later, Gale's ruling was reversed. The indictment of Belge would stand after all, and it appeared the beleaguered attorney might finally be required to stand trial.

The two-year battle neared its final resolution in late October. In addressing one of the most important cases ever brought before it, the Court of Appeals agreed to consider the charges against Francis Belge. New York State's highest court would now decide the issue once and for all.

Belge was back in the news in December for two reasons. The first involved a personal problem, a charge of harassment for forcibly entering the residence where his long-time girlfriend was staying. The county prosecutor requested that Belge be required to undergo a psychiatric examination.

Personally and professionally, his life was in turmoil, and things were spiraling downward. Though their relationship had been tumultuous at times, Belge's legal partner came to his aid. Frank Armani appeared as counsel on the harassment charge, asking the court to release Belge in his custody, with the assurance that Armani would take him for the court-ordered exam. The judge approved the request.

Then, just a few days before Christmas 1975, Belge's fortunes were reversed in spectacular fashion. Holcombe's relentless pursuit had finally been adjudged misguided and erroneous, as New York State's highest court dismissed the indictments against Belge by a vote of 6-1. The long battle was over, with Belge emerging victorious.

The concept of the attorney-client privilege remained intact. Frank Armani and Francis Belge were found to have acted properly in all of their dealings with Robert Garrow. They had stayed within the constraints of the law, and had maintained the confidentiality guaranteed their client.

In validating their actions as correct and responsible, the court reaffirmed an essential, though controversial, component of the American justice system. The case has since become a cornerstone of legal ethics courses across the country.

9

A Jailhouse Lawyer Cons the System

The story of Armani and Belge and the issue of privileged information was of great importance to the legal profession. It took more than a year before reaching final resolution, but during that time, Robert Garrow had not faded into obscurity.

Backtrack to the summer of 1974, when an unusual defense strategy ended with Garrow's conviction of murder in the death of Philip Domblewski. After admitting on the witness stand to seven rapes and four murders, Garrow was sentenced to a term of twenty-five years to life. He was imprisoned at Dannemora on July 2, beginning orientation while awaiting charges on the various crimes he had confessed.

On August 7, barely a month after sentencing, New York State's most notorious killer was back in court, this time in Syracuse. Appearing in Onondaga County, Garrow sought court-appointed representation for his upcoming trial on a number of charges, including murder.

The convicted killer wept before a packed courthouse, pleading with Judge Gale to allow his former attorneys to continue on his behalf. Of Armani and Belge, he said, "They are the only ones who showed me any understanding."

At the time, the lawyers were facing a barrage of criticism for not revealing the location of two of Garrow's victims, an important factor in the judge's decision. With reservations, Gale acceded to Robert's wishes. Seated in his wheelchair, Garrow responded to the judge in a low voice. "There were other people that knew what Mr. Armani and Mr. Belge knew."

Once again, Garrow had shocked a court audience, and there was more to come. When asked to elaborate, he said that a priest and a few psychiatrists had also known of the other murders he committed, prior to their disclosure in court.

Immediately, the press ran with the story, citing Judge Gale's reference to the disclosure as "a brand new bombshell." A major uproar followed, and it was suggested the grand jury might have to widen the scope of its investigation.

Though the psychiatrists remained silent, the priest in question spoke out two days later, confirming that he had met with Garrow, but never alone, and heard no details of any crimes. The matter was finally defused by an examination of the case record. The meetings did take place prior to Garrow's confessions on the witness stand, but well after the bodies of Petz and Hauck had been recovered by police.

In mid-September, Armani confirmed that the state appellate court had appointed him to prepare Garrow's appeal of the murder conviction in the Domblewski case. Armani added that he would likely again be partnered with Francis Belge.

As the year drew to a close, Robert Garrow once more captured the spotlight. On December 30, 1974, accompanied by three state police troopers, he left his prison cell in Dannemora for a very important trip.

The first stop was Elizabethtown. Appearing before Essex County Judge Charles Garvey, Garrow entered a plea of not guilty by reason of insanity in the murder of Susan Petz.

Then it was on to Lake George, before Judge John Dier of Warren County, where he entered an identical plea in the murder of Daniel Porter. Garrow was then returned to his cell in Dannemora.

On February 14, 1975, Garrow again left his prison cell, this time traveling to Syracuse. There, he stood before Judge Gale, who read his indictment by the grand jury on two charges of murder and one count of attempted first-degree rape in the death of Alicia Hauck.

The two murder counts included one for intentional murder and one for felony murder. Though there was one victim, New York State law allowed an additional felony murder charge for any homicide resulting from the attempted commission of a felony, in this case, rape.

Garrow entered a plea of innocent, and, at Armani's request, was remanded to the Public Safety Building in Syracuse. Instead of returning to Dannemora, nearly five hours away, he would be available for immediate consultation with his attorneys.

Four days later, the district attorneys of Essex, Hamilton, Onondaga, and Warren counties met. Discussions centered on the order of prosecution for crimes Garrow had admitted on the witness stand. There was also an exchange of information to help determine what other crimes he may have committed.

Garrow's next court appearance, scheduled for February 28, was unexpectedly postponed. The delay was curious, but the reasons remained veiled in secrecy.

Based on previous discussions among the district attorneys, it was surmised that prosecutors were still finalizing the sequence of legal actions scheduled against Garrow. Among the other possible reasons for delay was a plea bargain involving all four entities.

March 6, 1975, ended all speculation as Robert Garrow embarked on a brief legal journey unprecedented in New York State history. His first appearance was before Judge Ormand Gale in Onondaga County Court on charges of murder in the death of Alicia Hauck.

When Judge Gale asked for a formal plea, Garrow requested to address the court. "I would like to refer to myself as two different persons, 'Mr. X' and 'Mr. G.' Mr. X had no parents and nobody to show him what was right. I had this turmoil in my mind, this struggle between Mr. X and Mr. G."

Despite the turbulent inner conflict, Garrow said he still felt responsible for his actions, and pleaded for psychiatric care "to take this Mr. X away from me."

Once again, he may have committed crimes, but it wasn't his fault. The difference was, instead of periodic amnesia, the blame was now placed on the newly discovered "Mr. X."

Judge Gale asked Robert to clarify his plea, to which he responded, "I am guilty, your honor." Gale accepted the plea and imposed the minimum sentence of fifteen years to life.

The next day, Garrow appeared in Lake George in Warren County and pleaded guilty to the murder of Daniel Porter. Continuing to Elizabethtown in Essex County, he pleaded guilty to the murder of Susan Petz. The sentence in each plea was fifteen years to life, with all three terms to run concurrently.

It was all part of a deal worked out between Garrow's lawyers and the group of district attorneys. It was further agreed that any remaining charges pending in each county would be dropped. Added to the twenty-five-years-to-life sentence for the murder of Philip Domblewski, the plea terms were expected to keep Robert Garrow in prison for the rest of his life.

Following the court session in Elizabethtown, he was allowed a private meeting with several representatives of the local media. It was just another chance for Garrow to relieve himself of all accountability.

"I was running from another person in my life—he always could have my mind. Either inside, or I saw him at a distance. He was the person who kills. He had no conscience, no guidelines, nobody to train him or tell him what to expect as a result of his actions.

"A child learns and develops conscience. Nobody taught me. As a kid, I made my own rules and guidelines. I had nobody to tell me what was right or wrong as a child. I was put out to work at seven and a half years."

Just as he had done during court testimony, Garrow once again blamed others for his actions. He saw himself as a victim, never once expressing regret or dismay for the monumental pain he had brought to so many lives.

With all the legal maneuvering completed and all the cases closed, it would take more than a little time to heal the many wounds and incalculable suffering caused by Garrow's terrible life of crime. He could now return to his Dannemora cell to live out his days in anonymity.

Hardly. The ink was barely dry on the confessions when his name was once again splashed across the headlines. Westchester County, New York announced it was investigating Garrow for possible involvement in the murder of Troy schoolteacher Carol Segretta in 1960. Segretta was traveling to visit her parents when she was victimized by a roadside attack.

A passerby had stopped to help, and the killer ran off, leaving Segretta with multiple gunshot wounds. Witnesses assisted in putting together a composite drawing of the assailant.

When Frank Armani was asked about the possibility of Garrow's involvement, he noted that Garrow hadn't used a gun on any of his four victims. "I can understand them trying to make him a scapegoat. That's their job—to solve unsolved murders. But they should take a look at the modus operandi. I think the New York State police checked him out on twenty-two murders at one time or another."

The furor raised by the three guilty pleas and the investigation of Segretta's murder overshadowed another critical issue. Garrow still had an active appeal contesting his conviction in the murder of Domblewski. That case had not been included in the terms of the plea agreement.

While Armani and Belge prepared the appeal, their client was not sitting idle in Dannemora. Within weeks of his arrival, Garrow petitioned for a transfer to the Elderly and Handicapped Unit at Fishkill Correctional Facility, a medium-security prison an hour south of Albany, where he could receive proper treatment for his disabling injuries.

Shortly thereafter, the request was denied, setting off a maelstrom of events destined to embarrass and confound the entire New York State corrections system.

Rejection of the request was predictable, but Garrow would not be dismissed so easily. A convicted rapist and serial killer, facing a virtual life sentence in a remote maximum-security prison, would seem to have few options and little hope for the future. For the average prisoner, that might be true. However, this inmate was anything but ordinary.

Digging his heels in, he went immediately to work, and in late May 1975, Garrow made a blockbuster announcement: he had filed a lawsuit seeking $5 million in total damages from Frank Armani, Francis Belge, and Jon Holcombe.

Garrow was suing his own attorneys!

Belge was the hardest hit at $3 million, while Armani and Holcombe were targeted for $1 million each. (Quadruple the numbers for an approximation of value in 2009.) Belge was accused of violating his professional ethics by enlisting a friend, Ralph Kackison, to help locate Alicia Hauck's body. Armani was guilty of allowing Belge to act as he did, and Holcombe was charged with harassment of Armani and Belge, preventing them from devoting appropriate time to Garrow's defense.

Additionally, he claimed that all three lawyers used threats and extortion against each other, and as a result, Armani and Belge were forced to end the trial early. To represent him in court, Robert engaged the services of J. Byron O'Connell of Plattsburgh, considered by some the top trial lawyer north of Albany.

Garrow also filed papers with the appellate division of the New York State Supreme Court, asking that a special prosecutor be appointed to investigate the conduct of his Hamilton County trial. In other action, he petitioned the state supreme court for the right to inmate assistance in preparing legal papers.

Holcombe responded by applying to the state supreme court for a change of venue regarding the charges alleged by Garrow. The complaint originated in Clinton County, but all three attorneys cited in the suit lived and worked in Onondaga County, about five hours away.

In late June, the appellate division denied Garrow's bid for a special prosecutor to review the Hamilton County trial. But a few days later, Garrow earned his first victory of sorts when Supreme Court Justice Parker Stone rejected Holcombe's initial effort to move proceedings to Onondaga County. The court advised Holcombe that the appeal should have been submitted to Clinton County for adjudication.

A second victory was won by Garrow when State Supreme Court Justice Norman Harvey ordered officials at Clinton State Prison to comply with Robert's request that a fellow inmate be allowed to assist him in preparing court documents.

In late August 1975, Justice Harvey granted Holcombe's request for a change of venue, noting that all the parties except for Garrow were located in Onondaga County. Besides moving the action to central New York State, the judge ruled that Garrow would have to amend the lawsuit. By virtue of his office, Holcombe could be sued as a district attorney, but not as a private individual.

Garrow had nothing but time on his hands in prison, and

he had no intention of simply serving out his sentence. Every available minute was spent preparing legal papers, and in January 1976, Robert filed a request for reversal of his conviction in the Alicia Hauck case. He was again represented in court by O'Connell, a notoriously tough litigator.

The public was aghast. Garrow's case had already consumed enormous amounts of court time, ending with an admission of guilt and acceptance of a plea bargain in each of three murder cases. How could he appeal his own confessions?

In O'Connell's words, Armani and Belge "were looking out for their own skins" by allowing Garrow to take the stand and confess to other crimes during the Domblewski case. He further argued that the two attorneys had feared repercussions from withholding information about Hauck and Petz, and sought to derail misconduct charges by having Garrow admit to the murders. Said O'Connell, "There was no purpose in bringing these things out other than to exculpate themselves."

He cited pre-trial publicity as so pervasive that it prevented Garrow from receiving a fair trial. He also decried allowing the Domblewski photographs to be introduced as evidence. That decision was unwarranted, said O'Connell, since the only intent was to play on the emotions of the jury.

To rectify those legal lapses, he requested dismissal of the original indictment, or alternately, the right to a new trial. There was legal logic to O'Connell's arguments, and the appellate division of the supreme court agreed to consider his request.

In early February 1976, the court categorically rejected the assertions in Garrow's suit. On the charge that his attorneys urged him to confess on the stand, thus freeing them from possible prosecution, the court pointed out that Armani had, in fact, gone before the grand jury, and Belge was currently facing charges in the matter.

The justices also called it a reasonable strategy for Garrow to confess serious crimes and strange behavior in an effort to prove his insanity. As for pre-trial publicity, the court noted that trials are not held in a vacuum.

Addressing the issue of the crime-scene photographs, it was deemed unlikely that Garrow would have been acquitted without them as evidence. For those reasons, the court upheld his conviction in the Domblewski murder.

Just a few weeks later, Robert was at it again, filing papers in Onondaga County court, claiming his guilty plea in the Hauck case was a result of "trickery, deceit, fraud, and misrepresentation by the district attorney's office and defense attorneys."

Many of Garrow's court papers were handwritten, and as one assistant D.A. noted, "He's got more lawsuits going than any small law office." Robert even filed suit against his former doctor, claiming improper treatment of his injuries after he was gunned down, captured, and hospitalized in 1973.

In the Hauck case, he cited Armani's insistence that a guilty plea was necessary in order for Belge to present a successful defense. Garrow said he was "in a state of mental incapacity" when he made a "compulsory plea of guilty," and had been "terrified" into the guilty plea "by my attorneys and authorities."

And it didn't stop there. He charged the state with violating the terms of the plea-bargain agreement. In exchange for the guilty pleas, Garrow said, "I would receive preferential treatments, to wit: color television, free transportation for my wife and family to visit me, and confidential privileges, etc."

Garrow's suit also alleged he had been hypnotized by Armani, and that under hypnosis, he came to believe things that were, in fact, not true. "I had been hypnotized by attorney Armani [a claim confirmed years later by Armani], believing that I had committed many murders, including the Hauck murder. I am now certain that I did not murder the Hauck's girl."

In making that claim, he conveniently omitted any reference to the map and directions he had provided, allowing Belge to locate the body months before police found the remains.

On those grounds, Garrow filed a motion asking that his sentence in the Hauck murder be set aside. Judge Gale denied the motion, and reserved decision on Garrow's request for a hearing on the issues raised in his other court papers, including the rescinding of his guilty plea.

Whether or not any of Garrow's many lawsuits and motions were successful, they consumed an enormous amount of court time, requiring judges to review lengthy documents and issue rulings. Sometimes, additional responses were required from the D.A.'s office.

With the media coverage accompanying each legal filing, the public became more and more outraged. It was inconceivable that a multiple rapist and murderer could subject the courts to numerous lawsuits regarding crimes he had freely confessed while on the witness stand.

A month after his most recent filings, Garrow received news from Judge Gale's office. The request to withdraw his guilty plea in the Hauck murder case had been denied. In May, the Court of Appeals announced several more decisions affecting Garrow's attempts to have his murder convictions tossed out.

The state's highest court ruled that no further appeal would be accepted on the Hamilton County case involving Domblewski's murder. Since no significant question of law had been presented, Garrow's only recourse was to contest a constitutional issue. If he did so, the only remaining venue available was the United States Supreme Court.

Two weeks later, the state's leading jurists reached similar conclusions regarding Garrow's attempt to have the Hauck, Porter, and Petz murder convictions set aside. Each of Garrow's assertions was dismissed, and the overall finding was, "The issue cannot be reviewed again by this court."

That announcement ended the high court's willingness to look at Garrow's cases any further, but his battles were ongoing. He still had several motions pending in various county courts, seeking to reverse his earlier confessions and convictions that were part of the four-county plea bargain. Judges and attorneys were constantly forced to spend time on Garrow's many filings, all emanating from a tiny prison cell in Dannemora.

Robert simply would not acquiesce. Despite the high court's rulings, he again submitted papers seeking to reverse the Hamilton County conviction. In mid-August, the State Court of Appeals maintained its earlier position, refusing to hear any further arguments on the matter.

Of course, Garrow knew that even issuing a denial required the court to give the matter at least some attention. He happily remained an unrelenting annoyance at every level of New York

State's legal system.

In late November 1976, Garrow again burst to the forefront, filing an application for a $10 million civil suit with federal magistrate John McLane in Auburn. Submitted at the same time was an application to have the suit fees waived due to his poverty status, a move that was approved a few days later.

In the multi-million dollar suit, Garrow claimed Dr. Donald Kasprzak of the Champlain Valley Physicians Hospital in Plattsburgh had provided improper medical care, resulting in permanent injuries to his left foot. He accused the doctor of medical malpractice and negligence, and also named the hospital in the suit, claiming their failures might cause him to remain crippled and confined to a wheelchair "for the rest of my life."

The state police and Major Donald Ambler were named in the lawsuit as well. Garrow claimed that police pressured the doctor and the hospital to move him to another location before he had properly healed. Their impetus for doing so was defined as a fear of mob violence around the hospital.

To Plattsburgh residents, the concept of mob violence was laughable. The city of about 20,000 was generally considered laid-back, and the word "mob" was not even part of the vernacular. A few people quietly carrying signs protesting the recent Roe vs. Wade abortion ruling qualified as a massive protest by Plattsburgh standards.

Just a few months after the $10 million suit was filed, Garrow's other multi-million dollar action made the headlines. In February 1977, his attempt to have the $5 million claim against Armani, Belge, and Holcombe moved back to Clinton County was rejected.

In opposition to Holcombe's successful change-of-venue filing, Robert had counter-filed, claiming to be a Clinton County resident housed at Clinton Prison in Dannemora. The court disagreed, ruling that the three defendants lived in Syracuse, and Garrow still owned a home there, rendering Onondaga County the proper venue for the action.

Two weeks later, the four-time convicted murderer was on the attack again, filing a show-cause order against the New York State Department of Correctional Services. In the suit, Garrow demanded to know "why medical treatment, medical equipment, and rehabilitation were being denied." He contended that the situation was in violation of his constitutional rights under the Eighth and Fourteenth Amendments.

He further stated that such medical treatments were "denied to the plaintiff because of the plaintiff's crimes prior to being sentenced, which inflamed an enormous amount of animosity among the prison guards and prison officials, and under the circumstances, led the doctors, rightly or wrongly, merely to deprive plaintiff of any medical attention, leaving him to deteriorate and suffer and be subjected to all forms of harassment."

Also under the show-cause order, Garrow sought an explanation from the department as to why he had not been provided with "a motorized wheelchair or the alternative, a practical nurse."

In May, he won a pivotal victory when a state supreme court judge ruled that Garrow was entitled to see his own doctor. Attorney William Nelson of Prisoners' Legal Services said the decision would allow access to Garrow's state medical records, and perhaps verify that he was being denied treatment.

To comply with the ruling, the state arranged a physical examination at Albany Medical Center Hospital in late June 1977. Garrow's history of escape and trickery ensured he would be heavily guarded during the three-hour trip.

Since his incarceration at Dannemora, Robert had frequently complained of debilitating pain in his left side, the result of gunshot wounds sustained during his capture in August 1973. He remained wheelchair-bound despite the assurances from two doctors that he had healed.

The supreme court ruling opened a window of opportunity, allowing him to work towards obtaining an order for treatment and rehabilitation. A motorized wheelchair or a private nurse were starting to look like real possibilities.

An assessment covering strength, mobility, and dexterity was performed at Albany, after which Garrow was returned to his Dannemora cell. In late September, three months after the examination, New York's most famous and infamous criminal received some long-awaited news: he was being relocated.

Though it was not publicized at the time, the official reason for the move was a death threat against Robert at Dannemora. A fellow inmate, Royce Lamitie, claimed he had been offered $50,000 to poison Garrow. Prison management was skeptical of the supposed murder plan, but it provided a convenient cover story to explain Garrow's reassignment should the need arise. The transfer was completed with no fanfare.

The unofficial reason was quite different. Garrow had played the system to such effect that he had become an annoyance and an embarrassment to the corrections establishment. Granting his transfer request would finally shut him up and bring an end to the multitude of lawsuits.

He had won, but he wasn't entirely happy with the results. The request had been for transfer to Fishkill, but Robert was going to Auburn. Like Dannemora, Auburn was a maximum-security facility with no special accommodations in place for disabled inmates.

After sentencing on the Albany attacks in the early 1960s, he had managed an identical transfer, allowing Edith to easily visit him from Syracuse. But this time, being closer to family was not the goal. Garrow the litigant had more work to do.

As he prepared further legal action, Robert's name was bandied about in the campaign for Onondaga County sheriff. At issue was his period of incarceration in the Public Safety Building, where Garrow had been placed temporarily for psychiatric testing by Syracuse doctors.

Republican challenger John Dillon, once a Syracuse deputy chief of police, criticized sheriff's deputies for refusing to allow city investigators to question Garrow on thirteen sex crimes, including rape, while he was held there.

However, Dillon was conveniently ignoring one important fact. At the time, Armani had made it clear his client was not to be questioned by police. Garrow's sole purpose for being there was a court-ordered psychiatric assessment. As several political figures had done and would continue to do, Dillon was using Garrow's name recognition to boost his own public profile.

Within a month after his arrival at Auburn, Robert had

already pressured doctors there to support his transfer to Fishkill. The health director sent a recommendation to Albany, advising state corrections officials that Robert's physical needs could be better met at another facility, though Fishkill was not mentioned specifically. While Garrow awaited a response, he returned to preparing more legal papers.

In November, the state appellate court rejected Robert's attempt to have his conviction in the Hauck case set aside. He sought the move on the grounds that Judge Gale should have ordered a competency hearing before accepting Robert's guilty plea. The lawsuits just kept coming, limited only by Garrow's energy and imagination.

The $10 million suit against three parties—Doctor Kasprzak, the hospital in Plattsburgh, and Major Ambler of the state police—was still under consideration by a federal judge. Garrow's other allegations against the New York State police had been dismissed, but the remaining charges were voluminous, filled with a variety of accusations.

In the suit, Garrow claimed that negligence and conspiracy made it possible that he would be forever confined to a wheelchair. He charged that Dr. Kasprzak and Major Ambler, with "malice and wantonness, conspired to deprive Garrow of the necessity of orthopedic surgery that perhaps would have corrected the irreparable injuries sustained by Garrow as the result of damages to his left foot and left arm when shot during the manhunt."

He further claimed that his back was turned when he was shot, so Officer Leblanc "had no justified cause for shooting at him. Kasprzak wrongfully discharged Garrow from the hospital with a broken left arm and five .32 caliber slugs in his left foot, without timely orthopedic surgery."

He characterized his injuries as quite severe at the time, with "his arm still broken, the bones causing serious damage to the tissues, and a seriously damaged foot. The suffering was an act of torture beyond any standards of human endurance." The irony of that statement was enormous, coming from a murderer who had slowly, methodically knifed his victims to death.

Garrow added that he was deprived of medical treatment

for months at Dannemora, and that care was only administered when fellow inmates "complained because of the smelly odor given off by my decaying foot." With proper treatment, he said, "I would have been able to get around on crutches instead of being confined to a wheelchair for the rest of my life."

In early January 1978, U.S. District Court Judge Howard Munson issued a six-page report dismissing Robert's suit against Major Donald Ambler of the New York State police. The denial was based on the ruling that Garrow had filed the suit three days after the statute of limitations had expired.

The judge explained that the portion of the suit applying to Dr. Kasprzak was still active since the doctor had not moved for dismissal. Kasprzak was given thirty days to do so.

Just a few days later, the new health director at Auburn submitted a second recommendation to Albany, naming Fishkill as a more appropriate venue for Garrow to receive proper care. The counselor at Fishkill approved the plan "if he was paralyzed." For Robert, perhaps success was near.

Garrow's transfer to Auburn didn't slow his legal maneuverings, but instead gave him new targets. His latest filing was an extensive $1 million lawsuit against Auburn Correctional Facility, alleging improper treatment since his arrival there just five months earlier.

Named as defendants in the suit were State Corrections Commissioner Benjamin Ward; Auburn Prison Superintendent Robert Henderson; Auburn Prison Health Director Dr. Raul Aude; and Jerry Berry, first officer at Auburn's prison hospital.

In the seventy-four page suit, Garrow explained the reason for his transfer to Auburn, backed by inmate Lamitie's four-page statement describing the alleged plot to poison Robert at Clinton Prison. He then expounded on a multitude of situations involving serious infringement of his rights.

Among Garrow's contentions were: he had lost privileges in the move from Dannemora to Auburn; he was being "treated like an animal"; his bland diet was not being continued at Auburn; he was frequently fed seafood, despite the fact that prison officials knew it made him violently ill; meats and fruits served to him could not be eaten, since they were not peeled and cut as they were for other handicapped inmates; he had to use a manual typewriter (officials deprived him of the electric typewriter his wife had given him, saying it would place a strain on the facility's electrical system); he had been deprived of personal property, including a book on the subject of excessive prison sentences; his eight-track player and tapes were taken from him; and, that he didn't have appropriate shower and toilet equipment, causing him pain from the "strenuous procedures involved." As a grand finale, Garrow added that "plaintiff can show many deprivations herein, but it would take thousands of pages to present them to the honorable court."

Just as the massive lawsuit against Auburn was becoming public knowledge, word arrived in late February that he had finally attained his goal. The Albany staff had concluded Garrow was truly paralyzed and "would not present a security risk." His transfer to Fishkill Correctional Facility was approved. Robert Garrow had beaten the system.

In retrospect, his accomplishments were daunting. He had been the focus of one of the longest manhunts in American history. Following his capture and hospital recovery, there was the atypical trial strategy, culminating in his eventual admission of guilt to eleven major crimes.

After his subsequent conviction, the incredible tale continued with time served in the maximum-security prison in Dannemora; transfer to the maximum-security prison at Auburn; and transfer to the medium-security prison at Fishkill, but in the minimum-security section known as the Elderly and Handicapped Unit.

A dangerous killer, once adjudged to possess an I.Q. of 84, had pulled it all off in three and a half years. He had clogged the New York courts with multiple lawsuits and made a mockery of the New York State corrections system. And he wasn't finished just yet.

As usual, there was no public announcement of the move from Auburn to Fishkill. In fact, virtually no one was aware that Garrow had even left Dannemora.

In late August 1978, the remainder of Garrow's $10 million lawsuit was dismissed on the same grounds as the earlier ruling:

the statute of limitations had expired. The suit was considered a civil rights action, which had a time limit of three years. From the moment they were sent, Garrow's papers remained in transit for fourteen days before landing in the possession of the court, three days beyond the three-year deadline.

Dismissal of the $10 million suit due to an oversight seemed out of character for Robert, who had become well known for his fastidious legal work. With plenty of other lawsuits and motions pending in a variety of courts, something very unusual had gone unnoticed: Garrow had abandoned the chase.

Having attained his goal of transfer to Fishkill Correctional Facility, Robert had gradually withdrawn from his intense litigious schedule. He was finally in a place with the equipment and layout to properly care for handicapped inmates. The staff was efficient, and each day, corrections officers dutifully lifted Garrow in and out of bed, and assisted him on and off the toilet. His needs were being looked after in fine fashion.

And then he was gone.

10

Escape!

On September 9, 1978, at about 6:20 a.m., a Fishkill corrections officer was performing daily routine checks on the prisoner population. He could see inmate Robert Garrow lying in his bed, but when Garrow didn't respond to the officer's voice, further scrutiny was required. Robert hadn't risen during the night for a bathroom visit, and the last time he had been seen was about 10:30 the previous evening.

Closer inspection left the officer stunned. In Garrow's bed was a prison uniform, including shirt, pants, and hat. The uniform was stuffed with other clothing, and one pants leg was angled realistically to make it look like someone sleeping on his side. It was a dummy!

Where the hell was Robert Garrow?

A quick search was begun. Down the corridor from Garrow's room, past a guard's desk and through a door, was a porch. Tucked away in a corner of the porch was found Robert's wheelchair, covered by a blanket.

A feeling of panic began to set in among the officers. Fishkill had more than its share of escapees, but this was different. This was a prisoner from a maximum-security prison, New York State's most notorious criminal, and a man guilty of multiple rapes and murders. The guards had believed he was partially paralyzed, and now he had vanished.

The alarm was sounded and the search expanded. Soon it was determined that Garrow was not within the facility's buildings. Investigators again checked the porch where Robert's wheelchair was found. Attention focused on an inmate's shirt hanging from a broom handle. Closer examination yielded some disturbing news: the shirt concealed a possible exit point from the porch.

Behind the shirt, in a low corner, two of the decorative bars forming the porch screening had apparently been bent and then pressed back into place. The two metal bars masked a nine-inch-wide escape route. It hardly seemed large enough to accommodate a man the size of Garrow, about six feet tall and a huskily built two hundred pounds.

But that wasn't all. Further doubt was raised by other hurdles that awaited. Once through the bars, Garrow would have been confronted with a fence about fifteen feet high, topped with four strands of barbed wire. Beyond the fence, it was almost a half mile to the nearest outskirts of the prison compound. Had all those obstacles been somehow overcome by a partially paralyzed inmate? It did not seem at all possible.

State and local police were called, and soon the site was humming with activity. Searchers and bloodhound teams combed the extensive prison grounds, and helicopters hovered above. Roadblocks sprang up across the region. A powerful sense of déjà vu enveloped the scene, eerily reminiscent of the Speculator area five years earlier, and the subsequent events at Witherbee.

The search was on, and the target was familiar to citizens and lawmen alike. During the past five years, Garrow's face had become infamous across the state. Once again his name fairly screamed from bold headlines within New York's borders and far beyond. Déjà vu, indeed.

As the day wore on and Garrow wasn't found, phone calls were placed to many of the people who had helped send him to prison. Jon Holcombe, Norman Mordue, and William Intemann, all instrumental in Garrow's conviction, were notified by state police that Garrow had escaped. The men were warned to take whatever precautions they felt were necessary for their own safety and that of their families.

Said Holcombe, "I've been through many of these situations before, when I was in the D.A.'s office." Added Intemann, "I'm not particularly concerned. I don't think he'll be headed this way." "But," he added, "I'd hate to see what would happen to anyone he came in contact with."

When questioned by the press, defense attorney Frank Armani described Garrow as "a man with an IQ of 108 or 112, who functions better than most people who are geniuses. But he is a sick man."

Armani would later explain that he had real reason to be fearful, claiming a revenge hit-list had been found in Garrow's empty cell. The names Holcombe, Mordue, and Intemann were on it. At the top of the list were Frank Armani and Francis Belge.

The search for Garrow quickly became a full-fledged manhunt spanning Columbia, Putnam, and Ulster counties, all adjacent to Dutchess County, where Fishkill prison was located. A statewide alert was issued, with special concern directed towards Onondaga and Clinton counties, since Garrow had family ties in both areas.

A major thoroughfare, Route 84, ran parallel to the prison grounds. Little more than a mile away stood the tollbooths for the Beacon Bridge, which spanned the Hudson, and just across the river was the NYS Thruway. These were all very busy highways, where roadblocks at several locations now created massive traffic backups.

The most intense search was in the vicinity of the prison itself. There was still no evidence suggesting Garrow had successfully left the grounds, but there was also nothing to suggest he hadn't. His record of escape and evasion, combined with a vile criminal past, caused an icy chill to spread through the surrounding region.

Fishkill's locale was varied, with both urban and rural features adjacent to the prison site. Immediately to the east of the prison was a heavily wooded area, and a mile southwest lay Beacon, a city of thirteen thousand residents.

Perhaps most tantalizing to a desperate escapee was Interstate 84, just a short distance from the prison perimeter. If Garrow had made it to the main highway, he could be hundreds of miles away by now in any direction. Disaster might befall anyone he encountered.

Statewide, politicians were in an uproar. Democratic Governor Hugh Carey shared the headlines with Garrow, as criticism of the governor poured in from all sides. With the

Democratic state gubernatorial primary just two days away, the escape was especially ill-timed for Carey. His primary opponents were firing away unmercifully, hoping to unseat him.

Of course, for Republicans looking forward to November's polling, Garrow's escape was a spectacular pre-election gift.

While Carey called for a full investigation, his opponents sought the same. As details gradually leaked out, a story of ineptitude at all levels emerged. It became increasingly clear that Garrow's escape would have enormous, long-lasting repercussions across the state. For now, though, the focus was on catching a killer on the loose.

Fishkill's prison grounds had been searched thoroughly and repeatedly, with no results. Officials were puzzled how any inmate, let alone an injured or partially disabled one, had managed to vanish without a trace. The manhunt was portrayed as massive and statewide, and still there were no clues as to what had happened.

Later on Saturday, authorities revealed that, just hours before he disappeared, Garrow had telephoned his daughter. Police had already questioned her by the time the information was made public. A program at Fishkill allowed inmates to make occasional calls to relatives through the prison switchboard.

The calls were not monitored, so nothing was known about the actual conversation. That revelation alone, of inmate telephone privacy, astonished the public.

On Saturday evening a statewide bulletin was issued, alerting law enforcement to be on the lookout for a black 1978 Chevy Blazer reported stolen in Dutchess County, and possibly operated by Garrow. About an hour later, an update was issued regarding Garrow's description, noting that he might be using a hairpiece to cover his baldness, drastically altering his appearance.

On Sunday, the story took on more of the trappings of the Speculator saga. Garrow was allegedly sighted in Fishkill, in Albany, and twice in Syracuse. Once again, he had assumed the persona of a phantom criminal, appearing simultaneously at locations scattered far and wide. Police checked out each report, but none proved reliable.

Meanwhile, the prison grounds underwent several searches, sometimes by lines of officers advancing side-by-side. The Fishkill compound contained patches of intensely thick briars, some of it hardly fit for small animals, let alone humans. All but the densest, thorniest, sections were swept repeatedly by search teams. Officials soon admitted that they were fairly certain Garrow was no longer within the prison grounds.

The intense fear that had gripped the Adirondacks and northern New York in 1973 was revisited, this time felt in at least some way across the state and throughout New England.

A house-by-house search was begun in the city of Beacon, adding to the general panic spreading across the region. At the same time, more than two hundred police officers, including several teams with bloodhounds and German shepherds, searched within a ten-mile radius of the prison. Their combined labors remained unproductive.

With access to Route 84 at Fishkill, Garrow could easily be anywhere from Maine to Florida, or perhaps halfway across the country. Plus, he was a known killer and rabid sexual predator facing a life behind bars. He had nothing to lose.

Robert had now been missing for two days, and search leaders convened to reassess their strategy. A comprehensive inspection of all prison buildings Saturday night virtually eliminated the possibility that Garrow was secreted within the facility's walls.

Roadblocks, contacts in Clinton and Onondaga counties, and searches in the vicinity of the prison had failed to yield a single clue. Teams of law officers combed the seven hundred acres of forest adjacent to the prison, fully aware of Garrow's proven ability to remain hidden in the woods.

Three New York State police helicopters continued the hunt, assisting searchers as they once again concentrated their efforts within prison grounds and around the perimeter. Besides the various law enforcement officers engaged in the hunt, several units of the Corrections Emergency Response Team (CERT) had also been called in to assist.

Sing-Sing's CERT spent Sunday slogging through the bogs and tall grasses within the prison grounds. On Monday,

Greenhaven's CERT arrived to relieve them, while Fishkill's own CERT unit was at work around the clock. At times, as many as two hundred CERT members were probing the grounds at the same time.

Through Monday morning, not a single shred of evidence had been found to suggest where Garrow might be. The manhunt had entered its third day, and some officials voiced fears that their man was long gone.

Hundreds of law enforcement officers were involved in manning the roadblocks, operating the helicopters, following the bloodhounds, and searching in all directions for Garrow. Inside the prison, every probe had come up empty, but orders were to continue repeating the process.

On Monday afternoon, Greenhaven's CERT was assigned to conduct the third sweep through some of the thickest brush surrounding the compound. The prison's own men were still on the job, and at about 3:30 p.m., Fishkill CERT member Frank Lago found a small radio in a dense, brushy thicket filled with briars, located along the outside of the prison fence.

The Army Corps of Engineers had recently been at work on the site, and two new dirt roads bordered the area. It was assumed the radio belonged to one of the engineers. Closer examination revealed it was free of rust and still operational, somewhat surprising if it had suffered exposure to the elements.

One of the men recalled that a radio was among the personal items missing from Garrow's cell. The new evidence was sent to the Escape Command Center, and it was quickly determined that both the make and model matched Robert's radio. A further check of prison records, using serial numbers, provided confirmation. The radio was Garrow's.

Finally, a substantial clue. From the outset, his disappearance had been a complete mystery, but the radio placed him at a specific location. He still could be long gone, but now there might be a trail to follow. It was the first real break in the case, and officers pursued it immediately, knowing there was a possibility Garrow was concealed within the brushy area in front of them.

Other searchers were summoned, including Greenhaven's

CERT, which had just completed three sixteen-hour days of combing the grounds. Teams of thirty men each were posted on both sides of the brush, and a third squad covered the fence line. A number of other men were scattered across the area.

With a perimeter established, a state police bloodhound unit was called to the scene, arriving at around 5:30. The hope was to determine what path Garrow had taken since his disappearance on Friday night, and if, in fact, he was still in the brush.

One bloodhound led its handler into the heavy growth, and after emerging excitedly from a different location, another hound was put on the scent. When the second dog performed the same as the first, the scratched and bloodied handlers felt certain that Garrow had been there, and more importantly, that he was still hiding in the thicket.

The two search teams flanking the brush began moving in towards each other. They were all clad in orange jumpsuits, allowing them to track each other visually in such close surroundings.

It also meant they were easy targets for an armed subject, but officials knew that if Garrow had any weapon, it would be a knife, or a "shiv" of some type, posing little threat to the officers, some of whom carried firearms.

The two teams continued to close towards each other. Suddenly, Garrow was spotted, if only briefly. Now it was simply a matter of squeezing in on him for the capture. With sixty men approaching his position and others nearby, this would be an easy finish to a difficult search.

Again, Garrow was sighted, now lying on his stomach near a tree. An order was shouted out by a CERT officer: "Freeze!" A split-second later, searchers were stunned by gunfire coming from the brush.

Garrow had a gun!

The fugitive fired twice before officers opened up on their assailant. In a hail of gunfire, Garrow suddenly lay still. Unlike at Witherbee, this time he wouldn't be getting up.

Remarkably, though nineteen shots were sent in his direction, Garrow was struck by only four rounds, at least two penetrating the torso. His wounds proved fatal.

He had managed to get off five shots, one of them finding its mark, striking Dominic Arena of the Greenhaven CERT. When he heard the command to freeze, Arena believed that Garrow, just fifteen feet away, had surrendered. Instead, gunfire erupted, and in the first chaotic moment, he was hit in the thigh.

The bullet was deflected by his pelvis and settled into his other leg, causing considerable damage. Arena, unarmed, was pushed from the line of fire by a fellow officer while team members unleashed the fusillade that ended Garrow's life.

The strategy used to locate Garrow was credited to Captain Michael Halloran, who worked on the premise that Garrow would follow the same pattern of avoiding capture that he had used during the Speculator manhunt in 1973.

Then, Garrow had spent most of his time staying close to the highway, remaining hidden, but often able to observe his pursuers, and ready to grab a passing car as an escape vehicle. That information had also come from Garrow himself during trial testimony.

Five years earlier, it was Lieutenant Michael Halloran who was the first officer on the scene of the Domblewski murder, and who worked on the twelve-day manhunt, ending when Garrow was gunned down in Witherbee.

Lieutenant Halloran was now Captain Halloran. His efforts and experience were described as critical in bringing this final manhunt to a successful conclusion.

When word of Garrow's death reached the media, expressions of relief came from many sources. The primary players in Robert's 1974 trial summed up the feelings of most people, and it took few words.

William Hauck, father of Garrow victim Alicia Hauck: "Justice is served. He's gone. That's it."

Judge Ormand Gale: "Justice has been done."

Senior Assistant District Attorney Norman Mordue: "I'm glad we're through with him. I'm just relieved for all the people who had anything to do with him. The thing I'm sad about is that a corrections officer was wounded."

Frank Armani: "The tragic story is over with. I'm just relieved it's all over with and that no one else was killed. The families can sleep in peace."

Comment also came from Jon Holcombe, former Onondaga County district attorney, who described Garrow as the most dangerous person he had ever prosecuted. "It is a well-known fact in legal circles that Garrow was a suspect in fifteen other unsolved murders in upstate New York."

Mordue supported Holcombe's comments, adding that in two of those cases, the prosecution had extremely strong evidence against him.

Garrow's overall life of crime included four murders and at least nine rape victims, plus charges on multiple counts of robbery, endangering the welfare of a child, escape, attempted kidnapping, kidnapping, assault, criminal impersonation, possession of a deadly weapon, attempted rape, sexual abuse, and sodomy.

Many of the experienced lawmen who pursued him believed the number of crimes he confessed on the witness stand paled in comparison to the truth. He was, in fact, a major suspect in many, many other rapes and murders across northern New York. This vicious serial killer may well have been responsible for more than a dozen murders, and as many or more sexual assaults.

Those were secrets that Robert Francis Garrow took with him to his grave.

11

Answers, Changes

In the days following Robert Garrow's death, prison officials, corrections officers, politicians, police, the media, and the public all puzzled over the same questions. How could Garrow have escaped? How crippled was he? How could he remain hidden for so long? Where did he get the gun? Could he have been faking injuries while he was in prison? Why was he in a medium-security facility?

For most of those questions, evidence appeared lacking. Recognizing this, some officials voiced the opinion that several escape-related issues might remain forever shrouded in mystery. But that was nothing more than wishful thinking. Over time, answers began to trickle in, sending participants at all levels scrambling for cover and grasping for alibis.

And, once again, the Garrow story became a potent political football. There would be lots of blame-laying and passing the buck before the dust finally settled.

Some politicians and investigators hoped to control the release of information, but daily reports from multiple news sources kept them on their heels answering questions and confronting allegations. This was a story that wouldn't simply go away.

The media, emulating the new standard of investigative reporting established during the recent Watergate scandal, found obliging subjects at all levels. Many who had dealt with Garrow in some fashion were willing to talk, from neighbors to sheriff's deputies, prison guards, policemen, lawyers, judges, and state administrators.

When reporters asked about Garrow's mobility, Richard Hongisto, corrections commissioner-designate said, "It appears the best Garrow could do was drag himself." Such naiveté from a high-ranking official invited harsh criticism.

Somehow it hadn't occurred to Hongisto that Garrow's abilities had been sorely underestimated, considering all the obstacles he had overcome. The empty wheelchair, the bent bars, the high fence, and the fact that he managed to avoid detection for three days suggested Garrow was capable of far more than just dragging himself.

Soon it was widely reported that not only could Robert walk, but that a trooper at the shooting had seen Garrow running. When that headline story appeared, it was time for damage control, and officers on the ground were quickly muzzled.

State police troopers were ordered to refrain from further comment on the case, and to refer all queries to the main office in Albany. On the following day the trooper retracted his statement, claiming he had said no such thing about Garrow being able to run. When pressed, he suggested an off-hand comment of his might have been misinterpreted. The newspaper stood by its original story "100 percent."

Fishkill Superintendent Theodore Reid asked to speak personally to anyone claiming they had seen Garrow moving about, effectively quelling any similar stories coming from corrections officers.

It was reported that Reid had earlier sent memos to superiors in Albany, asking that Garrow be moved from Fishkill to a more secure facility. Reid initially denied those claims, but later admitted he had indeed complained about Garrow being held there, portraying it as typical behavior among all superintendents. When a particularly dangerous criminal was assigned to their facility, they routinely voiced objections.

Attacks were launched at Florence Frucher, assistant deputy commissioner in charge of the classification and movement of prisoners. It was Frucher who had authorized Garrow's transfer from Auburn to Fishkill. She arrived at that decision based on the opinions of three doctors who had examined Garrow. They assessed him as an immobile inmate, a hemiplegic suffering paralysis on the left side of the body, and said Auburn did not have the facilities to meet his needs.

Critics pointed out that Frucher, whose husband was the director of communications for Governor Carey's re-election campaign, had no experience or training in corrections when she was handed the appointment. Carey's people fired back that Frucher was largely a transfer agent, and was more than qualified for the position.

William Gard, deputy commissioner for corrections facilities, stepped into the fray. Gard said it was his decision to allow Garrow's transfer to Fishkill, and with the same information given to him now, he would do it again. And so it went.

As the political battle raged, prison officials were still busy trying to figure out how Garrow had pulled it off. Fishkill, however, was no stranger to escape. Garrow's mysterious flight for freedom had been the third breakout in the past three weeks. In fact, the prison's two most recent escapees were believed to have hidden in the same thickets that Garrow had used.

Remarkably, there was even a precedent for handicapped prisoners escaping. Two years earlier, a pair of inmates on crutches had managed a similar feat. However, they weren't totally dependent on the crutches, which were found abandoned along the perimeter fence. The men were later recaptured.

The bigger issue was that a dangerous criminal like Garrow belonged in a maximum-security setting, but had somehow wheedled his way into Fishkill, a medium-security venue with a record of frequent escapes. Due to his supposed infirmities, he had been housed in the wing for the elderly and the handicapped, the most lax setting in the entire facility. The litigious Garrow had certainly done his homework in seeking a transfer to Fishkill.

Prison management faulted the officer who was on duty when Garrow escaped. Had he been seated at his station, Garrow couldn't have moved about without being noticed. The guard was suspended without pay, but the corrections labor union jumped to his defense, charging management with using him as a fall guy to cover the prison's own shortcomings.

The issue became politicized. Union officials cited the need for more officers, claiming the guard in question was performing other duties when Garrow passed down the corridor unseen. In their view, increased staffing would have prevented the problem.

It seemed as if everyone was pointing the finger at someone else, and no one was interested in accepting any blame.

Hongisto stepped into it again, this time speculating that Garrow couldn't have escaped without a key to the fence surrounding the prison. That suggestion brought unity, in a sense, as both labor and management officials at Fishkill took offense at his remarks.

The intimation was that some lapse on their part had allowed Garrow to obtain a key. Many characterized Hongisto's comments as an effort to find a scapegoat, and to direct attention away from any responsibility he might bear.

Even Governor Carey tried to put a good spin on the story, claiming that Garrow hadn't actually escaped, since he was killed on prison property. Theoretically and factually, it would have taken a great leap of faith for voters to accept that analysis. He was ignoring the fact that police and corrections officers described the area of the shooting as "just beyond state property lines," within easy reach of Route 84.

Carey took it even further, adding that Garrow's violent end was a good lesson to others in jail who might consider trying to escape. That, too, was a tough story to sell, considering Fishkill's deplorable escape record, and his own unwavering stance against capital punishment.

For the second consecutive year, Carey had vetoed a bill that would have restored the death penalty in New York State. Each time, he narrowly avoided an override, and Republicans now smelled blood in the water, portraying him as soft on crime, and offering the most recent escape from Fishkill as proof. Instead of wending his way through the corrections system, they said Garrow should have been sitting on Death Row.

The governor continued his efforts to play down the case, saying it had now become nothing less than a political tool for his opponents to use in the upcoming election. Whether or not that was true, the effects were unmistakable. Five days after Garrow was killed, the *Syracuse Post-Standard* ran an editorial detailing the considerable damage to Carey's re-election campaign from the effects of the escape fiasco.

Discussed were widespread criticism of his anti-death-penalty stance, the possibility of a cover-up, and the innumerable unanswered questions about Garrow's transfers and escape. Among the conclusions reached was that Carey was in real trouble, and that the manifold Garrow issues could potentially derail his campaign.

The discontent among rural voters was assessed concisely: "If the election were to be this next Tuesday, instead of on Tuesday, Nov. 7, there seems little doubt that Perry B. Duryea, Jr., the Republican nominee for governor, would win in a landslide upstate."

While the political posturing continued, corrections officials concerned themselves with the particulars of the escape. The weapon that Garrow used to shoot Dominic Arena was a source of much attention. It proved to be an old, foreign-made firearm of very poor quality, yet still operational, a .32 caliber Gaztanaga Destroyer pistol made in Spain in the early 1900s. It fit into the general category of cheap handguns referred to as "Saturday night specials."

Superintendent Reid said it was certain the gun had not been smuggled into the prison. Frisking, metal detectors, and hand-held scanners were used on all visitors and packages, rendering it impossible for the pistol to have been carried into the prison undetected. In fact, Garrow's inmate visitor card required that all of his callers face an additional check with the hand-held scanner.

It was believed the gun had instead been planted from the outside. The main highway and the surrounding landscape offered plenty of opportunities.

Reid was particularly vexed by the lack of evidence suggesting the route Garrow had followed. He noted that, of all the steps necessary to escape, negotiating the lofty fence was the least likely.

Could he have climbed a fifteen-foot-high fence topped with four strands of barbed wire? Others had done it in the past, but pieces of clothing or bits of blood and skin tissue were always left behind. In Garrow's case, there was nothing. The fact that he was far less than able-bodied made the issue even more perplexing.

The porch was examined closely, with hopes of solving the

mystery of how Garrow might have created the opening that he eventually squeezed through. A likely scenario was decided upon, and a re-enactment simulation was ordered. Officials put men to work on breaking through the bars, which took them approximately twelve minutes. They determined that Garrow had used a table leg to break the bars, and then wriggled his way through.

Theoretically, none of that could happen in a medium-security prison. But medium-security was merely the overall rating of Fishkill, a grading based on the type of fencing and obstructions used to keep inmates confined. Robert had been held in a minimum-security wing of the overall medium-security facility. In terms of confinement, it was light years away from the unyielding walls of Dannemora, a fact that he was well aware of.

Another major issue to address was the actual extent of Garrow's physical impairment. Six weeks after he was shot and captured at Witherbee in 1973, Garrow had been pronounced healed, with no signs of any disability. Respected Plattsburgh physician Dr. Donald Kasprzak arrived at that conclusion, and Dr. Dick's assessment of the defendant during the trial at Lake Pleasant confirmed Kasprzak's diagnosis.

And yet, for five years, Robert had remained in a wheelchair, pushed or carried everywhere by sheriff's deputies, corrections officers, and fellow inmates.

As it turned out, Garrow had been examined fifty-three times by a number of physicians, all with varying results. Twenty of those sessions addressed his supposed paralysis. In Robert's lawsuits, he omitted the findings of doctors who concluded there was no apparent reason for any immobility.

Other findings that were less than accurate and much more supportive of Garrow's claims became tools that he used in seeking prison transfers. Now, corrections officials blamed the doctors, and the doctors blamed corrections officials. The buck was passed so often that it would take months to sort it all out.

The final word on the extent of Garrow's incapacity would be determined by an extensive lab study of his body tissue, begun shortly after the autopsy. Conclusions from the testing were expected to be available within two months.

Besides the official investigations, the media was hard at work delving into Garrow's background. Their efforts yielded illuminating commentary from a variety of lawmen who had dealt with him since his incarceration in 1973. Garrow had served time at Dannemora and Auburn prisons, the Hamilton County Jail, and the Public Safety Building in Syracuse. His former keepers had much to say.

Among the comments made in reference to Garrow were: "a con artist"; "not surprised he escaped"; "a good faker"; "he didn't move like a deer, but he moved"; "a pain in the neck, killing us with kindness and preying on our sympathy"; and, "a malingerer." One officer called him "a polished actor. When he had an audience, he played a role."

Several lawmen from different sites noted they had seen Garrow standing, or taking a few steps. No one at Auburn or Fishkill saw Robert out of his wheelchair, but there were rumors he had been secretly exercising. And perhaps not so secretly. In what now appeared to have been physical training for the escape effort, it was reported that Garrow had used an exercise bar above his bed in the weeks prior to his disappearance.

Some Fishkill employees did notice Garrow had very well-developed shoulders. He was known to possess strength far above the average man, as had been noted by friends and employers during his time in Albany in the late 1950s.

In the days following the escape and shooting, official investigations were almost as varied and numerous as Garrow's lawsuits once were. The New York State police, the corrections department, the county district attorney's office, and the Senate Committee on Crime and Correction were all conducting separate inquiries, besides Fishkill's own internal investigation.

And, of course, the criticism of Governor Carey and the political patronage system was emphatic and persistent. Persons with no history of involvement in the corrections system were holding prominent, powerful, well-paid positions. The qualifications of several appointees were subjected to public scrutiny, and many were called into question.

A week after Garrow was killed, and several days after his burial, Robert once again made the headlines in rather ghoulish fashion. In huge, bold type, newspapers proclaimed, "Doctors Preserve Garrow's Brain."

Medical professionals explained that Garrow's brain, plus some nerve and muscle tissue, would help determine his physical capabilities, which were a statewide issue with potential electoral implications. The battle for governor of New York State could well be determined by the outcome of the tests. Carey's opponents savored the possibilities.

A great uproar arose with the announcement that final autopsy results, including brain and tissue testing, were expected by mid-November, coincidentally just one week after the elections. The political bickering intensified, and accusations flew from both sides.

Even after he was gone, it seemed Robert Garrow was still managing to throw a wrench into the system. He may have been dead and buried, but his legacy of manipulation was alive and well, and prospering.

Meanwhile, in the absence of definitive answers regarding Garrow's unlikely saga, the verbal attacks escalated amidst charges of wrongdoing at many levels. In an effort to quell the uproar, Dutchess County District Attorney John King announced the matter would be investigated by a grand jury. Among the issues to be addressed was whether or not the killing of Garrow was justifiable homicide.

At the same time, the state Department of Correctional Services had an announcement of its own. Building 13, the minimum-security section of Fishkill, would soon be closed "until such time as the department's security review is completed and recommendations for increased security have been adopted."

The inmates held at Building 13 were scheduled for transfer, and a new facility for elderly and handicapped inmates was planned, though the location was as yet undetermined.

The search continued for evidence that would explain how Garrow obtained the gun he used against corrections officers. Records showed that the last family member to visit him was his son, Robert, Jr., on September 2 and 3, about a week before the escape. Since Garrow's death, police had questioned family members repeatedly, but gleaned little information.

The investigation continued, and by late September, persistence paid off, culminating in four arrests. Despite assurances to the contrary by high-ranking prison officials, police indicated the gun had indeed been smuggled into the prison after all. There were suggestions it may have been concealed within a container of food.

It was also noted that Garrow's wheelchair should have set off a metal detector, but officers might have ignored the alarm since it was a frequent occurrence. Due to ongoing investigations by other groups, troopers withheld further comment.

Arrested in connection with the escape were Robert Garrow, Jr., of Syracuse; Doreen Sciabica of Franklin Square, Long Island; Doreen's husband, Vincent Sciabica of Fishkill Correctional Facility; and Raymond Loftus, also a Fishkill inmate. Vincent Sciabica and Raymond Loftus had both been assigned at times to push Robert around in his wheelchair.

Garrow, Jr., 18, and Mrs. Sciabica, 26, were held in the Dutchess County Jail after their arraignment, while the two inmates were arraigned within prison walls. The twenty-seven-year-old Sciabica was serving five to fifteen years for first-degree manslaughter. Loftus had been imprisoned for a maximum of four years on charges of second-degree assault.

Police investigators had solved many parts of the puzzle, but details of the prison escape didn't emerge officially until young Garrow's court appearance on September 29. Standing before Dutchess County Judge Raymond Aldrich, Jr., he admitted to carrying a .32 caliber pistol in a bucket of chicken, and explained how it was done.

Robert Garrow, Sr., had devised the gun-smuggling plan with fellow inmate Sciabica, whose cell was next to Garrow's. Sciabica's wife, Doreen, brought the gun to young Garrow, who was staying in a motel near Fishkill. Though he knew she was bringing some chicken, he claimed in court to be unaware she was also carrying a gun until she showed it to him and told him of the plan.

Robert, Jr., said the gun, described as a 7.65 mm, ten-shot pistol, was wrapped in a plastic bag. He placed it at the bottom of the bucket, under the chicken, and intentionally spilled gravy on it to make certain the inside of the container was messy.

The next day, September 3, he paid a visit to the prison, passing several times through metal detectors while the bucket of chicken sat on a bench. An officer did ask what was in the container, but didn't look inside it himself. (The officer's union later claimed a guard did peer briefly into the bucket, but didn't dig to the bottom.)

Garrow then shared a picnic table with his father in the visitors' area. No mention was made of the hidden contraband. As they relaxed and chatted, Robert, Sr. carefully masked removal of the pistol and secreted it between the seat of his pants and the wheelchair.

While they ate, Garrow, Sr. explained that he had planned and arranged the details of the smuggling effort. At some point, he managed to tape the gun to his thigh, where it passed undetected during a pat-down before he left the visitors' area. A week later, he executed his escape plan.

After confessing the story to the judge, Garrow, Jr., pleaded guilty to one felony charge of promoting prison contraband, which carried with it a potential sentence of seven years. In exchange for the guilty plea, two misdemeanor charges were dropped. He was released on $5,000 bail, pending sentencing in late October.

Garrow's accomplices, the Sciabicas, were charged with promoting prison contraband, plus the two misdemeanor charges of conspiracy and illegal possession of a weapon. They pleaded innocent on all counts.

In a bit of positive news, Dominic Arena, the officer shot during the capture of Garrow, Sr., had recovered from his wounds, and received the Medal of Valor from the Department of Corrections. Fishkill CERT member Frank Lago was also cited, receiving a medal for "meritorious performance of duty." It was Lago who discovered Garrow's radio, leading to the end of the manhunt.

In the meantime, officials at all levels of the corrections hierarchy were called to testify in a variety of venues. Investigators had tenaciously dug deep into Garrow's past, tracking everything from Dannemora to Fishkill. The disturbing conclusion was inescapable: Garrow had duped nearly everyone.

The multitude of lawsuits he had filed were all part of a plan.

The picture that emerged from events of the past five years portrayed a wily, manipulative inmate on a mission. Beginning with papers filed from his Dannemora cell, Garrow worked both the legal and correctional systems, gaining expertise from stacks of law books. Frequent failures did nothing to discourage him.

For the next four years Robert filed a dizzying array of lawsuits, targeting men of power and position. He even sued his own attorneys. At any given time, he had a half-dozen active suits, occupying resources from county courts all the way to the New York State Court of Appeals.

At first he was an annoyance, and then a major nuisance. But all along it was a smokescreen, masking his goal of placement in a less-secure facility. The key, of course, was to pass himself off as disabled, a ruse he maintained for five years.

Doctor after doctor had examined him, with some doubting the veracity of his complaints. But Garrow knew there was safety in numbers. By visiting so many physicians, he convinced several that his incapacity was legitimate.

Taking full advantage of the bureaucracy, and answering each rejection with a more potent counterpunch, he achieved his goal. If only he had applied such persistence to a good life, instead of a life of crime.

The story was embarrassing to Governor Carey, but also to New York's entire correctional system, which had been exploited by the worst of the worst. Ineptitude, naiveté, ignorance, and arrogance were all revealed as details of the case unraveled.

Immediately following Garrow's death, several officials had quickly stepped forward and accepted a measure of responsibility, only to be chastised by political opponents for attempting a cover-up, a term popularized in the Richard Nixon era.

There was some truth to those allegations. The perception was not uncommon: an official anxious to admit mistakes very likely had something else to hide. By acting quickly, it was hoped the story would be put to rest.

It was a path many politicians had followed successfully in the past, but was now trumped by media cynicism. Reporters were driven to probe for details rather than accept statements at face value.

Every media member was a skeptic, and public figures were often left with three choices. A story could be told in their own words, in the words of a friend or enemy who chose to talk, or in the words of a reporter. But a story would be told. The ultimate effect was one of checks and balances, and, in the end, transparency.

Surprising details emerged, sometimes from the upper echelons of government. For the public, among the most disturbing aspects of the case were personal communiqués between Garrow and a top prison official.

Warren Harding, an assistant inspector general for the corrections department in 1978, was one of the original investigators involved when Robert requested a transfer from Auburn to Fishkill. Surprisingly, Harding's own testimony confirmed that Garrow had offered to abandon his $10 million lawsuit, contingent upon a transfer.

It was disturbing enough to learn that a lowly rapist and murderer enjoyed direct communications with a high-ranking corrections administrator. But it was nothing short of stunning that a criminal could leverage his way out of a bad situation into a prison of his own choosing. All appearances indicated that was exactly what had happened.

Harding said Garrow was moved from Auburn because he needed medical care, not because of his proposal to abandon litigation. Still, it was confirmed that once he arrived at Fishkill, Garrow had dropped the large lawsuit, along with several others, and focused his efforts on developing an escape plan.

That made it an especially tough sell for the public, the media, and the Senate Committee on Crime and Correction to accept Harding's claim that dropping the lawsuits was merely coincidence, unrelated in any fashion to the transfer.

Harding insisted the move was justified because Auburn simply was not equipped for long-term care of handicapped inmates. Pressed further, he said, "I realized the man had a point. How can we expect him to spend the next twenty years there? At the time, I said, 'If Garrow takes us to court, we're going to lose.' " That statement alone validated the effects of

Garrow's pervasive legal actions.

Harding's argument was less than convincing, and its veracity soon came into question. Senator Ralph Marino stunned the committee, reading portions of a letter from Harding to Garrow, confirming that his transfer to Fishkill was forthcoming. One snippet suggested some arm-twisting may have been involved. Wrote Harding: "It took a bit of explaining. I suggest that you keep a low profile. Don't let me down."

The transfer was made, the lawsuits stopped, and Garrow quietly settled into life at Fishkill. He had certainly upheld his end of the bargain. Until, of course, he vanished.

The effect of that revelation was jaw-dropping, to say the least. The realization that an assistant inspector general had performed the bidding of one of the most notorious murderers in New York State history was chilling. That type of intimate, direct contact between a high government official and a brutal killer left a feeling of uneasiness among the public.

And, as Benjamin Ward, former head of the corrections department, pointed out, wheelchair-bound inmates were being held at that very same time in Attica, a maximum-security prison. If they could manage, then so could Garrow.

Whatever the case, and despite Harding's claims to the contrary, Robert's incessant lawsuits had served their purpose. Without them, he might still be in Dannemora. His shrewd strategy of using legal filings to obtain transfers, either blatantly or subtly, had worked.

He had fooled doctors, prison administrators, and psychiatrists, and faked his way through the system. And, once he reached Fishkill, the medical lawsuits against the state were dropped, even though Garrow received no different therapeutic treatment at Fishkill than he had at Auburn or Dannemora.

In early November, the case against Robert Garrow, Jr., was resolved. His attorney read a letter to the court, which said in part, "There were times when I wondered if I ever had a father. When I saw my father in prison, I only thought about how much I wanted him out. From the very beginning, he would ask me to help him get out."

The judge granted him youthful offender status and imposed

a sentence of up to four years at the State Division for Youth in Elmira. The penalty was comparatively light, intended as an opportunity for young Garrow to get a new start in life.

Judge Aldrich told him, "Your name is Garrow, and wherever you go, you will be ridiculed and taunted. You must live with that forever."

He also offered advice and encouragement: "You have everything going for you, Robert, except your father's name. I think the sooner you get rid of it, the better you'll be. Your father's death was his own doing. He died as a result of his own violent acts, and you shouldn't think for one minute that you're responsible for your father's death."

It would be some time before he could accept that viewpoint. During the manhunt, the Garrow home in Syracuse had been under surveillance, and inside, young Robert anxiously awaited any news. An officer assigned to monitor the home said the family was watching television when a report came through that Garrow had been killed.

Robert reportedly "went wild," storming angrily from the house and knocking the screen door off its hinges. That ending to his father's story was not what he intended, and there was no denying his role in the outcome, despite the judge's assertions.

Final resolution of the remaining escape-related charges came several months later, in March 1979, when both Sciabicas reversed earlier stances and entered guilty pleas. Vincent told the court that Garrow had threatened to harm his wife and children, and ordered Sciabica to have Doreen pick up a gun and deliver it to young Robert at the motel.

After the new pleas were entered, Vincent was returned to his cell in Greenhaven, and Doreen was released in her own recognizance. Three weeks later, she was sentenced to five years probation, having already served six months in jail while awaiting trial. Vincent was given two to four years at Sing-Sing Prison in Ossining, New York, but the penalty was ruled concurrent, adding nothing to his overall sentence.

At about the same time, an autopsy report was released, confirming about Robert Garrow what many suspected, and what officials had admitted: there was no evidence of any paralysis.

Doctors said a determination of that fact could have been made years ago if Garrow had simply been taken to a neurologist.

It was also discovered that he had a broken collarbone, likely suffered when he cleared the high fence beyond the porch. Officials speculated that he may have fallen, and the injury may have impeded Robert's efforts to escape the prison perimeter.

Garrow's story would have repercussions for years to come, but several changes were made soon after his death, some at Fishkill, and some statewide. As early as mid-October, many adaptations and revisions had already taken place. The department of corrections was well into a review of the case histories of 5,940 prisoners statewide. Since Garrow's escape, 156 inmates had been identified as high-risk and had been moved to higher-security facilities.

The investigations had revealed many systemic problems running the gamut from corrections officers all the way up to statewide administrators. Though blame wasn't placed solely on the officers, it was noted that if Robert Garrow, Jr., was telling the truth about smuggling the gun in to his father, then it was obvious that officers had not used proper search procedures.

At Fishkill, food from outside was no longer allowed into the facility, and the inmate strip search required after meeting with visitors was strictly enforced. Two officers on horseback were assigned daily to patrol the prison perimeter from dawn until dusk. The nearly impenetrable thickets bordering Fishkill's expansive grounds were removed, and a series of personal alarms was installed, along with two entry posts.

The prison's fencing system was revised, starting with the eighteen-foot-high section that Garrow had climbed. The strands of barbed wire along the top were replaced by the much-less-forgiving barbed tape. Outside of the main fence was added a second fence, eight feet high. Coils of barbed wire were placed between the two barriers.

All visiting areas were combined into a single unit, and plans were made to install a closed-circuit TV monitoring system. Officials were paying long-overdue attention to improving the facility, which to some observers had become a correctional sieve. In the past five years at Fishkill, there had been sixteen incidents of escape involving thirty-five inmates. Garrow's story had exposed that deplorable record to the public, and it was now deemed unacceptable.

Statewide there were many policy revisions. An Escape Review Board was created to analyze each breakout attempt, with periodic reports detailing possible improvements. In the Inspector General's office, an Escape-Absconder Unit was formed to coordinate search and recapture missions.

A new position of Security Review Specialist was created in the Office of Classification and Movement, the department responsible for recommending Garrow's transfer. To monitor the process, Management Analysis Teams were formed.

Revision of the procedures for identifying and classifying inmates was begun, and a plan was made to computerize all records to increase efficiency and make information available in a timely fashion. Corrections also requested the complete hospital records of all inmates receiving treatment outside of prison facilities.

Robert Garrow had turned the system on its ear, affecting every administrator, every corrections employee, and every inmate in the state. The repercussions were likely much more far-reaching, as corrections departments in other states moved to prevent similar occurrences.

In 1978, an uncommonly transparent self-analysis was published. The Department of Correctional Services issued an official ninety-six page report entitled *The Escape of Robert F. Garrow.* Many of the findings were both startling and embarrassing.

After examining the case from start to finish, state investigators concluded that:

- Garrow had been examined by doctors more than fifty times in five years. Many of those assessments were described as cursory, cited by the report as "very crude examinations."

- Medical assessments performed within short time spans often resulted in directly opposing conclusions, ranging from "considerable atrophy" to "no evidence of atrophy."

- Garrow's multiple lawsuits were believed to have been a contributing factor in obtaining transfers.

- The Dannemora "assassination plot" was likely a fabrication.

- Within four months after Garrow's reassignment to Auburn, medical officials there applied twice to Albany for another transfer, the second request specifying Fishkill.

- Albany medical staff and corrections officials agreed that Garrow was truly paralyzed and "would not present a security risk."

- Subsequent events proved that Garrow was not paralyzed and that the premise for his transfer was erroneous.

- Poor record-keeping played a role throughout Garrow's years of incarceration.

- "Garrow's manipulation of lawsuits to buttress his self-serving claims of paralysis, and to exert pressure on the medical staff to take the path of least resistance by not disputing his claims" led to a fragmented, inaccurate medical history.

- After only five months at Auburn, Garrow was transferred to Fishkill.

- Once Garrow was at Fishkill, the lawsuits stopped. He pronounced satisfaction with the medical care he was receiving in the Elderly and Handicapped Unit.

- Despite praising his care at Fishkill, "medical records on Garrow's confinement show he received no therapy for his alleged paralysis," and that any treatment he received was available at any maximum-security facility.

- Security at Fishkill was poorly enforced.

- Despite claims that Garrow's body was riddled with bullets, nineteen shots were fired at him by four officers, with only four bullets finding their target. Garrow fired five shots.

By 1980, much of the dust had finally settled, and Robert Garrow's story began to fade from prominence. It resurfaced in 1984, when Frank Armani told his tale in a book entitled *Privileged Information*. Tom Alibrandi co-authored the book, a dramatized version of the case, focusing on the difficulties faced by Armani and Belge as they sought to define and maintain lawyer-client confidentiality.

Armani's book claims he gave information to searchers at Fishkill that ultimately led to the discovery of Garrow's hiding place. If that was true, it was puzzling why he didn't provide them with other, potentially life-saving, information.

The following excerpt was published in the *Syracuse Herald-American* the day after Garrow disappeared, and while the search was ongoing:

> Armani last night said he was "shocked" by Garrow's escape—"shocked that he had the ability to escape, and the opportunity." He said he believed Garrow's disability was real, because the gunshot wound left Garrow's Achilles tendon severed and shortened, and his left arm had atrophied.

More than three years earlier, in January 1975, Garrow was supposedly wheelchair-bound at Dannemora. In the presence of his attorney, he had stepped free of the chair, revealing the ability to use his legs. He then lowered himself to the floor and performed several one-armed pushups, demonstrating for Armani the strength he had built from exercising during six months of incarceration. Armani never told anyone of the incident.

With three years to further develop that strength and the ability to walk, Garrow was almost certainly more of a danger than ever when he arrived at Fishkill. But when asked to comment during the search in 1978, Armani passed on the opportunity to mention Garrow's potential mobility.

There are striking differences between the two assessments. While promoting his book, Armani was asked about the incident at Dannemora, to which he replied, "I'm not going to answer that. I just thank god. I could have lived to regret that day."

It was a curious response, coming from an attorney lauded for his historic stand in defense of ethics.

The only inference to be drawn from "I could have lived to regret that day" is that someone could have been seriously injured or killed because Armani had withheld potentially critical information about Garrow's condition.

In fact, after the display viewed by Armani at Dannemora, all lawmen guarding Garrow for the next three years were in more peril than they realized. They were not handling a disabled, paralyzed prisoner, which is naturally done in a more relaxed fashion. That's why facilities like the Fishkill Elderly and Handicapped Unit existed.

Unlike the missing bodies issue, revealing Garrow's deceit and malingering might not have violated any oath, since it had no bearing on the Domblewski case or any other pending charges. But that is a gray area in the realm of legal ethics. Garrow's fakery held great potential for further crimes like assault against guards or attempted escape.

He confirmed that potential by fleeing from Fishkill, nearly killing a corrections officer in the process. Several search team members could have lost their lives that day when Garrow unexpectedly opened fire on them.

Was there reasonable certainty those crimes would be committed? Perhaps. More than anyone, Armani was aware of Garrow's proclivity for violence and his history of escape, and mentions in his own book Garrow's escape plans during the Hamilton County trial.

It also appears Garrow perpetrated a major fraud when he filed the $10 million suit against doctors, the hospital, and police, seeking damages for injuries he said would keep him confined to a wheelchair for the rest of his life.

Even though Armani did not represent Garrow in that

lawsuit, perhaps the attorneys' oath exempted him there, too, from revealing what he knew. If so, it's unfortunate.

The underlying premise allowing Garrow's eventual transfer to Fishkill was his disabling injuries, and only he and Armani knew the truth about their severity, or lack thereof. Had Garrow's fake or exaggerated medical claims been exposed at the time, he may never have left Dannemora.

During a book tour, Armani described his infamous client. "I was convinced he was a schizophrenic person. One Robert Garrow I did not like at all. He was a very dangerous person.

"There was one Robert Garrow who was very considerate of his family, was a hard-working man, and took his god-given talents and operated at full capacity. Another one was a brutal bastard who treated people as things."

Two years after publication, the rights to *Privileged Information* were purchased by 20th Century Fox. Armani said he was "wined and dined" in Hollywood while a deal was worked out, and he received "a substantial fee."

In 1987, the story of Garrow's lawyers was the basis for a TV movie entitled *Sworn to Silence*, starring Dabney Coleman, Peter Coyote, and Liam Neeson. Coleman won an Emmy for his portrayal of Francis Belge, and the movie received many fine reviews. The story's details were changed, using a Pennsylvania location, and the names were altered.

The subject also received serious coverage by Fred Graham, legendary broadcaster and attorney. Graham was the CBS news law correspondent for fifteen years, covering the Supreme Court and all facets of the United States legal system. He appeared regularly on national television, including the CBS Evening News. He has also been highly visible since the early 1990s working for Court TV (now truTV).

Among the documentaries Graham put together in his career was a 1987 television special entitled *Ethics on Trial*. The lead story for that program was the Robert Garrow case, and the conduct of Armani and Belge was examined.

Frank Armani participated in the show, and when asked by Graham if even "scum like Garrow" was entitled to full protection by the lawyer's code, he replied, "If it doesn't hold for the worst of us, then it shouldn't hold true for the best of us."

In an interview later, Graham added, "I think Armani did the right thing, but I'm certainly glad I wasn't in his shoes. Once he was told this information, he was stuck. The surprising thing is that Garrow trusted him enough to tell him this. Most lawyers would not get this kind of information.

"Often, there seems to be a winking relationship between lawyers and crime. They don't want to know about it."

Garrow's story surfaced again in 1991 when Armani and Alibrandi's book, *Privileged Information*, was released in paperback. Over the years, the case has become a staple in law courses across the country. Students struggle with the complex question of ethics, trying to determine what Armani and Belge should have done. Almost invariably, after examining all of the angles, they come to the conclusion reached by the two Garrow attorneys years earlier.

Not everyone agrees with the path the lawyers chose, particularly the public. The perception is that criminals are coddled, given rights far beyond what they are entitled to, and far beyond what they allow their victims.

That clearly was the impression of the average citizen who watched Garrow admit to multiple rapes and murders, and then toy with the legal system for years. No one will ever know how many women he raped, or how many people he killed. He victimized many with his violent nature and unfeeling acts, and manipulated people from all walks of life.

Garrow's story prompted fear, amazement, revulsion, and disbelief. People across New York and beyond were mesmerized by the initial manhunt, the details of his trial, and the story of his escape. For the better part of five years he captured the headlines, carving a reputation as one of the state's most notorious criminals ever.

That is the legacy of Robert Francis Garrow.

Epilogue

Of the many cases in which Garrow was a suspect, five received much media attention and have been mentioned on websites and in newspaper articles: Martha Allen, Karen Levy, Joanne Pecheone, Carol Segretta, and Ruth Whitman. Two of those cases were solved when Levy's murderer confessed in 1975, and Segretta's did so in 1977.

Ruth Whitman's boyfriend was an initial suspect when she was found beaten to death in Colonie in December 1959. He denied involvement and was released. Two years later, he was convicted of beating a man to death in Canada and sentenced to life in prison. New York State BCI officers interviewed him after his conviction, but he maintained his innocence in Whitman's death. Garrow lived in the Albany area and was considered a suspect.

A badly decomposed body found floating in Black Creek, north of Syracuse, in August 1973 (see page 63) was eventually identified as Martha Allen. The twenty-one-year-old Allen "looked like she was fifteen," according to her grandfather, whom she lived with. The cause of death was undetermined, and the case remains unsolved.

Circumstances suggested the possible involvement of Garrow. Analysis of his murders confirms that Garrow killed when he felt intense mental pressures, whether real or imagined. For instance, his appearance on the Geddes charges was scheduled for July 12. On July 11, he raped and killed Alicia Hauck, and then skipped his court appearance, committing two more murders within the next few days.

Coincidentally, that court appearance was rescheduled for July 26. It was on July 25 that Martha Allen was last seen alive. Garrow, who nearly never missed a day of work in his life, did not attend work on July 24 and 25. In the next few days, he attempted the abduction of three young girls at Speculator, and then kidnapped the four campers, murdering Domblewski.

In January 1972, Joanne Pecheone, a nineteen-year-old high school student from Utica, was found half-clothed and tied to a tree. She had been raped, and died of multiple stab wounds. Those four major components of the crime sounded like a blueprint for Garrow's rapes and murders.

Utica was one of the locations said to have been found on a map in Garrow's car, one of twenty-seven places specially marked in red ink, perhaps indicating the locations of his rape and/or murder victims.

In 2009, the Allen and Pecheone homicides are still actively investigated among central New York's cold case files in the hopes that modern forensics might finally solve the crimes.

Illustration Credits

Gooley, Lawrence P. and Jones, Jill C. Page 112 (map).

Jones, Jill C. Page 111 (top) 2006.

New York State Archives. Page 110 (top, middle, bottom), 111 (middle, bottom).

People of the State of New York against Robert F. Garrow, Sr., Official Court Record, June 17–27, 1974. Evidence Photographs. Page 106 (top, bottom). 1973.

Syracuse Newspapers Photo Archives. Page 105, 106 (middle), 107 (top, middle, bottom), 108 (top, bottom), 109 (top, bottom).

Bibliography

Alibrandi, Tom and Armani, Frank H. (1984) *Privileged Information*. New York City, NY: Harper Collins.

People of the State of New York against Robert F. Garrow, Sr., Official Court Record, June 17–27, 1974.

People v. Belge, 50 A.D.2d 1088, 376 N.Y.S.2d 771 (1975).

People v. Belge, 83 Misc. 2d 186, 372 N.Y.S.2d 798, 803 (1975).

People v. Belge, 50 A.D.2d 1088, 376 N.Y.S.2d 771 (4th Dept. 1975), aff'd, 41 N.Y.2d 960, 390 N.Y.S.2d 867 (1976).

State of New York, Department of Corrections, *The Escape of Robert F. Garrow*. 1978.

(newspaper bibliography on pages following)

Bibliography - Newspapers

"Area man last victim of serial killer." Gloversville Leader Herald, August 24, 2008.
"Local happenings." Ticonderoga Sentinel, April 10, 1947.
"Michalak's tavern ad." Ticonderoga Sentinel, October 26, 1950.

Plattsburgh Press-Republican
"Adirondack search turns up no leads." August 3, 1973.
"Garrow case spurs death penalty interest." September 15, 1978.
"Garrow case under microscope." September 13, 1978.
"Garrow killed in shootout." September 12, 1978.
"Garrow kin would have turned him in." August 11, 1973.
"Garrow moved from CVPH." September 20, 1973.
"Garrow: people locked doors." August 8, 1993.
"Garrow pleads guilty." March 8, 1975.
"Garrow pleads in Essex killing." February 15, 1975.
"Garrow readies suit on CVPH, others." November 24, 1976.
"Garrow says he feels relieved." February 15, 1975.
"Garrow capture harrowing experience." April 13, 2008.
"Manhunt cost taxpayers money." August 11, 1973.
"Manhunt spurs local tension." August 8, 1973.
"Mountain man dead." September 13, 1978.
"The greatest manhunt in NY history." August 8, 1993.
"William Gebo." February 19, 1952.

Syracuse Herald-American
"Court to review Belge indictment." October 31, 1976.
"DA will reply to ethics queries." June 23, 1974.
"Decision due in suit by Garrow." October 2, 1977.
"Garrow book polishes old memories." July 8, 1984.
"Garrow hits medical care." February 23, 1977.
"Garrow lawyers ordered to defend." June 16, 1974.
"Hauck girl's remains found." December 9, 1973.
"Records of Garrow subject of hearing." August 19, 1973.
"Slotnick claims DA is playing politics." August 18, 1974.
"Troopers press woods manhunt." August 5, 1973.
"Upstate notebook: Garrow is dead." October 8, 1978.
"Woman's body found may be Garrow link." December 2, 1973.

Syracuse Herald-Journal
"$5 million legal action." June 22, 1975.
"200 Hunt Garrow." August 4, 1973.
"A look inside Garrow's cell." September 13, 1978.
"Alicia's family still has hope." September 12, 1973.
"Alternate still lacking." June 8, 1974.
"Appeals court denies Garrow bid." June 26, 1975.
"Armani before jury." February 7, 1975.
"Armani book." July 8, 1984.
"Armani cleared in Garrow case." February 7, 1975.
"Armani grand jury." September 13, 1974.
"Armani may be subpoenaed." February 22, 1975.
"Assault on 2 girls denied by Garrow." October 18, 1973.
"Attorney declines comment on gravesite." August 14, 1974.
"Attorney to undergo psychiatric exam." December 10, 1976.
"Belge complaint squashed." February 12, 1975.
"Belge filed complaint against DA." February 11, 1975.
"Belge has until Tuesday to answer charges." February 14, 1975.
"Belge indictment dismissal upheld." December 20, 1976.
"Belge indictment ruling reversed." January 16, 1976.
"Belge loses bid to arrest DA." March 4, 1975.
"Belge ordered to stand trial." March 28, 1975.
"Belge's immunity hearing Tuesday." February 28, 1975.
"Body-finding lawyers have officials baffled." June 20, 1974.
"Both sides offer arguments in ethics case." August 5, 1974.
"Call to account." June 21, 1974.
"Camper's slayer hunted." July 30, 1973.
"Candidates agree." October 14, 1977.
"Charge son got gun to Garrow." September 20, 1978.
"Code prevented telling of bodies." June 19, 1974.

"County DA aide to assist at Garrow trial." April 22, 1974.
"County to empanel extra grand jury." July 16, 1974.
"Couple who aided Garrow sentenced." June 8, 1979.
"Court rejects Garrow bid to overturn." February 6, 1976.
"Court upholds Garrow convictions." May 21, 1976.
"DA counters motions." August 1, 1974.
"DA files papers on Belge immunity." February 20, 1975.
"DA knows of no action on plea bargain." June 22, 1974.
"Dangers abound for conservation force." September 1, 1973.
"Garrow arraigned in death of Alicia." February 14, 1975.
"Denies office aware of bodies." July 13, 1974.
"Don't quiz Garrow, police told." January 8, 1974.
"Escape has Governor Carey in hot seat." September 11, 1978.
"Escape still a mystery." September 13, 1978.
"Fees waived for Garrow suit." November 30, 1976.
"Four cases in area murder links sought." January 4, 1974.
"Four counties join forces for murder probes." January 4, 1974.
"Fresh men hunt Garrow." August 6, 1973.
"Garrow admits 3 slayings." June 18, 1974.
"Garrow admits 3rd killing." March 7, 1975.
"Garrow admits killing." March 6, 1975.
"Garrow admits undisclosed rape." June 17, 1974.
"Garrow appeal denied." May 6, 1976.
"Garrow appeals denied." May 21, 1976.
"Garrow appearance postponed." February 6, 1975.
"Garrow arraignment expected tomorrow." October 17, 1973.
"Garrow asks for reversal of conviction." January 9, 1976.
"Garrow attorneys' case." October 14, 1974.
"Garrow buried, investigation continues." September 15, 1978.
"Garrow case analyzed." February 19, 1975.
"Garrow case to be probed by grand jury." July 3, 1974.
"Garrow defense objects to 8 photos." June 12, 1974.
"Garrow denies guilt by reason of insanity." December 31, 1974.
"Gale denies motion to question jurors." August 6, 1974.
"Garrow escape still a mystery." September 30, 1978.
"Garrow escapes." September 9, 1978.
"Garrow faces new hearing." October 23, 1973.
"Garrow faces new testing." January 8, 1974.
"Garrow faces trial in assault." July 12, 1974.
"Garrow files new plea to overturn verdict." February 26, 1976.
"Garrow found wounded in prison cell." November 21, 1973.
"Garrow gets hearing date on lawsuit." April 6, 1977.
"Garrow given 25 years to life." July 1, 1974.
"Garrow goes to Dannemora." July 2, 1974.
"Garrow hunt turns to car." August 7, 1973.
"Garrow insane defense claims." June 27, 1974.
"Garrow jury completed." June 9, 1974.
"Garrow jury filled." June 4, 1974.
"Garrow jury hunt continues." May 13, 1974.
"Garrow jury hunt to enlarge." May 16, 1974.
"Garrow jury selection to end." June 3, 1974.
"Garrow jury still one short." June 7, 1974.
"Garrow lawyers face jury probe." July 3, 1974.
"Garrow lawyers may plead insanity." June 10, 1974.
"Garrow leaves questions." September 12, 1978.
"Garrow lying about amnesia doctor says." June 24, 1974.
"Garrow lying psychiatrist says." June 24, 1974.
"Garrow maintains silence." August 11, 1973.
"Garrow may have gotten pistol in food." September 21, 1978.
"Garrow on trial." May 8, 1974.
"Garrow: others knew of victims." August 7, 1974.
"Garrow panel selection begins." May 29, 1974.
"Garrow photos posted at police roadblocks." August 9, 1973.
"Garrow pieces things together." June 18, 1974.
"Garrow plans appeal." September 13, 1974.
"Garrow attorneys claim case prejudiced." August 24, 1973.
"Garrow rejected." April 1, 1976.
"Garrow remains at large." September 11, 1978.
"Garrow ruled fit for trial." February 9, 1974.
"Garrow searchers ring area." August 3, 1973.

Bibliography

"Garrow seeks $1M for rights violation." March 14, 1978.
"Garrow sentenced." July 2, 1974.
"Garrow serving term in Dannemora." July 2, 1974.
"Garrow sister testifies he had cut on his hand." June 20, 1974.
"Garrow sly faker." September 21, 1978.
"Garrow sought by 200." August 4, 1973.
"Garrow sues lawyers, DA." May 21, 1975.
"Garrow suit moved." August 26, 1975.
"Garrow suit rejected." January 5, 1978.
"Garrow to see his own doctor." May 4, 1977.
"Garrow to stand trial." March 6, 1974.
"Garrow trail proves elusive." August 8, 1973.
"Garrow trial continues selecting jurors." May 14, 1974.
"Garrow trial move pondered." April 25, 1974.
"Garrow trial move rejected." April 26, 1974.
"Garrow trial: prosecution completes case." June 14, 1974.
"Garrow trial ready to start." May 8, 1974.
"Garrow trial winding up." June 26, 1974.
"Garrow undergoes checkup." June 24, 1977.
"Garrow victims known to others." August 8, 1974.
"Garrow will enter two more guilty pleas." March 7, 1975.
"Garrow's cell now empty." September 13, 1978.
"Garrow's lawyers baffle officials." June 20, 1974.
"Garrow's pistol center of attention." September 14, 1978.
"Garrow's publicity rapped." August 22, 1973.
"Garrow's trail cold." August 8, 1973.
"Garrow's trial nears beginning." June 6, 1974.
"Grand jury ruling due on attorneys." September 6, 1974.
"Harris confesses to Levy murder." July 28, 1975.
"Harris gets 20-life in Levy murder." September 24, 1975.
"Haven't read affidavit, judge says." February 27, 1975.
"Hauck case to go before grand jury." November 14, 1974.
"Hauck clue explained: police - someone knew." June 21, 1974.
"Hauck father files complaint." June 24, 1974.
"Hauck slaying: Garrow pleads innocent." February 15, 1975.
"Holcombe attempts fails to shift suit by Garrow." July 3, 1975.
"Holcombe counters Taikeff's charge." July 13, 1974.
"Hongisto: Garrow at Fishkill a mistake." September 21, 1978.
"Hunt for Garrow narrowing down." August 3, 1973.
"Indictment of Belge overturned in court." August 1, 1975.
"Inmate, wife admit helping Garrow flee." March 14, 1979.
"Inquiry." July 5, 1974.
"Jail guard doubled: Garrow denies guilt." September 20, 1973.
"Judge approves fee claims; praises 2 lawyers." July 29, 1975.
"Judge hunts jurors for Garrow trial." May 21, 1974.
"Judge rejects Garrow lawsuit against doctor." August 25, 1978.
"Judge will instruct Armani grand jury." September 13, 1974.
"Jury candidate pool now at 105." May 24, 1974.
"Jury pool at 97." May 23, 1974.
"Jury pool completed." May 25, 1974.
"Karen Levy's body reported found." October 26, 1974.
"Law checked on Garrow's lawyers." June 24, 1974.
"Lawyer case tries strategy." July 23, 1974.
"Lawyer given court subpoena." February 5, 1975.
"Letters to editor." June 26, 1974.
"Levy's remains to be buried." October 31, 1974.
"Lid on lawyers' case." June 25, 1974.
"More trials for Garrow." June 28, 1974.
"Mother believes missing daughter dead." August 16, 1973.
"Motions weighed in Garrow trial." June 11, 1974.
"No trace yet of missing girl." July 24, 1973.
"North Country priest denies told of victims." August 9, 1974.
"Panel hears judge in Garrow case." November 20, 1974.
"Police hope to quiz Garrow." December 3, 1973.
"Police push manhunt for suspected slayer." August 1, 1973.
"Police scour woods for hint of Garrow." September 11, 1978.
"Police search heavy woods for teen's killer." July 31, 1973.
"Possible Garrow link to 5th slaying probed." March 8, 1975.
"Potential jurors nervous during screening." May 10, 1974.
"Pressure beat Garrow." August 10, 1973.

"Priests, psychiatrists meetings." August 8, 1974.
"Prison chiefs subpoenaed." September 22, 1978.
"Prosecution hits Garrow lapses." June 19, 1974.
"Prosecution in trial of Garrow continues." June 13, 1974.
"Psychiatrist has version of stabbing." June 21, 1974.
"Recall murder case and manhunt." August 2, 1973.
"Rural judge ready for trial." May 13, 1974.
"Search stirs resort town." August 1, 1973.
"Secrecy clamped on lawyers' case." June 25, 1974.
"Sentencing for Garrow set for today." July 1, 1974.
"Shirt spurs search." August 2, 1973.
"Show looks at ethical issues and the law." January 20, 1987.
"Slotnick criticizes Holcombe." August 28, 1974.
"State bar president urges better ethics." July 3, 1974.
"Summaries due at Garrow trial." June 27, 1974.
"Suspect identified, police stalk teen's killer." July 31, 1973.
"Suspected slayer sought 3." August 2, 1973.
"Tells of cost." June 29, 1974.
"Ten picked in Garrow trial." June 1, 1974.
"Tough row to hoe: Garrow given 4 years ." November 3, 1978.
"Troopers continue manhunt." August 7, 1973.
"Two named to Garrow trial jury." May 30, 1974.
"Two officers honored in Garrow capture." October 6, 1978.
"Upstate notebook: Garrow is dead." October 8, 1978.

Syracuse Post-Standard
"3 DAs map out Garrow probe." July 12, 1974.
"A story of a reign of terror." June 20, 1984.
"Armani to head appeal." September 13, 1974.
"Armani's Privileged Information." June 20, 1984.
"Asks jury quiz in lawyer case." July 24, 1974.
"At death, relief replaces outrage." September 12, 1978.
"Auto stolen in manhunt." August 7, 1973.
"Await tests on Garrow." December 1, 1973.
"Bodies pawns in plea bargaining." June 22, 1974.
"Burial rights counts filed against Belge." February 14, 1975.
"Carol Segretta killer confesses." March 24, 1977.
"Confirm firearm charge dropped." January 8, 1974.
"Conflicts arise in confidentiality issue." August 16, 1974.
"Court refuses to hear Garrow appeal." August 13, 1976.
"DA aide studies laws, asks probe of lawyers." June 25, 1974.
"DA hints Garrow able to walk." September 20, 1978.
"DA opposes insanity plea." June 11, 1974.
"DA points to precedent in case against lawyers." July 6, 1974.
"DA ties Garrow to Alicia Hauck's death." July 4, 1974.
"Death would be better." June 28, 1974.
"Decision on tapes awaited." September 11, 1973.
"Denies Holding 2 As Captives." November 14, 1972.
"Dr. Szasz comments on insanity plea." August 16, 1974.
"Drops quest." November 15, 1972.
"Editorial: Garrow effect on Carey." September 16, 1978.
"Face sentencing in Garrow case." March 15, 1979.
"Film firm buys rights to murder story." April 12, 1986.
"Final juror seated." June 5, 1974.
"Fishkill guard charged in Garrow escape." September 18, 1978.
"Fourteen added to Garrow jury pool." May 22, 1974.
"Garrow remains silent." August 13, 1973.
"Garrow a suspect in theft of knife." July 31, 1973.
"Garrow admits stabbing youth." June 18, 1974.
"Garrow: another charge." March 8, 1975.
"Garrow appeal planned." June 28, 1974.
"Garrow asks exam." October 24, 1973.
"Garrow attorneys probe: new bombshell." August 8, 1974.
"Garrow begins prison sentence." July 3, 1974.
"Garrow called his daughter." September 10, 1978.
"Garrow charged in death; back in court." March 4, 1975.
"Garrow continues to evade pursuers." August 1, 1973.
"Garrow decision Tuesday." June 29, 1974.
"Garrow files suit, claims mistreatment." March 7, 1978.
"Garrow found guilty in slaying." June 28, 1974.

"Garrow given 25 years." July 2, 1974.
"Garrow unaware of slaying consequences." June 22, 1974.
"Garrow here for tests." January 15, 1974.
"Garrow jurors total seven." May 31, 1974.
"Garrow kin freed on $1000 bail." August 14, 1973.
"Garrow less than an animal." June 23, 1974.
"Garrow loses appeal bid." February 11, 1977.
"Garrow murder trial testimony." June 27, 1974.
"Garrow questioned on memory lapses." June 20, 1974.
"Girl, 17, reports assault." September 27, 1969.
"Garrow rational, witness testifies." June 12, 1974.
"Garrow seeking change." August 6, 1975.
"Garrow shot and captured." August 10, 1973.
"Garrow slain in shootout." September 12, 1978.
"Garrow slips by police roadblocks." August 8, 1973.
"Garrow status unchanged." August 30, 1973.
"Garrow story may be book." February 18, 1975.
"Garrow suing for injuries." November 24, 1976.
"Garrow testing awaited." December 14, 1973.
"Garrow to leave hospital, go to jail." September 15, 1973.
"Garrow too late." October 4, 1978.
"Garrow trial adjourns." May 11, 1974.
"Garrow troubled, dangerous." September 11, 1978.
"Garrow was con artist." September 17, 1978.
"Garrow won't talk to police." January 18, 1974.
"Garrow's attorney urging surrender." August 8, 1973.
"Garrow's murder trial opens." May 9, 1974.
"Garrow's son, 3 others charged." September 21, 1978.
"Garrow's son admits giving gun to dad." September 30, 1978.
"Garrow's trial begins Wednesday." May 5, 1974.
"Gravy covered Garrow's gun." November 14, 1978.
"Hearing slated." February 23, 1974.
"Holding Garrow costly." March 25, 1974.
"Hongisto to appear at escape hearing." September 28, 1978.
"Hunt continues for killer." August 1, 1973.
"Hunt Garrow near sister's." August 9, 1973.
"Hunters searched thickets." September 14, 1978.
"Judge hears motions in probe of attorneys." August 6, 1974.
"Jury sought in Garrow slaying trial." May 10, 1974.
"Lab after clues." August 25, 1973.
"Lawyer cleared in Hauck case." February 8, 1975.
"Lawyer to claim Garrow insane." January 20, 1974.
"Legal ethics revolting." June 20, 1974.
"Letters to editor." June 25, 1974.
"Letters to editor." June 27, 1974.
"Meehan going after gougers." June 29, 1974.
"Metro briefs: state denies Garrow appeal." November 5, 1977.
"Murderer Garrow still at large." September 11, 1978.
"Mysteries of escape still unsolved." September 15, 1978.
"New Jersey law journal defends lawyers." July 29, 1974.
"Okay Garrow as youthful offender." November 3, 1978.
"Plea-bargained over bodies." June 22, 1974.
"Police intensify hunt for camper's slayer." July 31, 1973.
"Police lacking leads in probes of deaths." September 10, 1973.
"Police probe coed's death." December 3, 1973.
"Possible suspect in Martha Allen murder." April 4, 2004.
"Potential jurors selected." May 14, 1974.
"Prisons: Garrow saga ends." December 30, 1978.
"Prosecution rests case in Garrow murder trial." June 15, 1974.
"Prosecution rests." June 15, 1974.
"Prosecution's turn in Garrow trial." June 24, 1974.
"Psychiatrist doubts truth of Garrow tale." June 26, 1974.
"Psychiatrist told press of Garrow." June 25, 1974.
"Reign of terror: author's dilemma." June 20, 1984.
"Rejects plea for mistrial." June 13, 1974.
"Report on Garrow called coverup." October 21, 1978.
"Return 8 indictments: one may cite Garrow." August 22, 1973.
"Review: Privileged Information." June 20, 1984.
"Robert Garrow used lawsuits to get transfer." October 20, 1978.
"Ruling expected on Alicia's death." December 10, 1973.

"Sardino plans probe of lawyers." June 20, 1974.
"Search woods in Camillus." August 3, 1973.
"Senate panel opens Garrow probe." September 15, 1978.
"Shirt hoped a clue." August 2, 1973.
"Sister treated Garrow cut." June 21, 1974.
"Six armed troopers to escort Garrow." September 19, 1973.
"Six more potential jurors." May 16, 1974.
"Tearful Garrow cannot recall." June 19, 1974.
"Tests begun." January 16, 1974.
"The full story behind Garrow." October 22, 1978.
"The Garrow story." June 20, 1984.
"Tormented lawyer finds peace." August 21, 1989.
"Trooper saw crippled Garrow run." September 13, 1978.
"Troopers close in on slaying suspect." August 1, 1973.
"Troopers get nowhere in questioning." August 12, 1973.
"Two jurors selected for trial." May 30, 1974.
"Warrant for DA may be opposed." February 12, 1975.
"Week-old manhunt continues." August 6, 1973.

Troy Times Record
"Boyfriend of slain area girl convicted." November 17, 1961.
"Killer still denies part in girl's death." November 25, 1961.
"Man arrested on six counts." November 6, 1961.

Index

S

Sacandaga River 32, 38
Saratoga County, NY 56
Sardino, Thomas 146
Schiller Park 120–21
Sciabica 191–92, 196
Segretta, Carol 160–61, 204
Senate Committee on Crime and Correction 189, 194–95
Sharland, Emma 88
Sherwood, Kenneth 13–15
Silver Hill Road 55–56
Sing-Sing Prison 177, 196
Slotnick, Melvin 149–50
Speculator, NY 3, 14–16, 19, 24, 27–29, 31–35, 38, 40–43, 45, 47–55, 60, 67, 74, 84, 131–32, 134, 174, 176, 180, 204
Spencer Street 120
Staincamp, Francis 37, 39
State Industrial School 99–101
Stone, Parker 148, 162
Supreme Court 77, 148, 150, 153–54, 162–63, 165, 167, 202
Sworn to Silence 202
Sylvan Beach 63
Syracuse, NY 19, 24–25, 34, 43, 49, 51, 53–54, 60–61, 63–64, 66–67, 70–72, 76, 115–16, 118, 121–24, 128–29, 131, 141–42, 146–47, 157–59, 166, 168, 176, 186, 189, 191, 196, 200, 204
Syracuse University 24, 70–71, 76, 123

T

Taikeff, Elliot 147–50
Teeple, Fred 28
Ticonderoga, NY 97, 99
Tracy, Jan Mary 21
Troy, NY 102, 104, 160
Tupper Lake, NY 52

U

Ulster County, NY 175

V

Vodron, John 13–14, 83